CRITICAL THINKING SKILLS:

PRACTICAL TOOLS FOR RATIONAL THINKING AND DEEP ANALYSIS TO BOOST YOUR BRAINPOWER. ADOPT LOGIC STRATEGIES TO FIND INTELLIGENT AND EFFECTIVE SOLUTIONS TO CHALLENGES.

© **Copyright 2019 - All rights reserved**

The content contained within this book may not be reproduced, duplicated or transmitted without direct written permission from the author or the publisher.

Under no circumstances will any blame or legal responsibility be held against the publisher, or author, for any damages, reparation, or monetary loss due to the information contained within this book. Either directly or indirectly.

Legal Notice:

This book is copyright protected. This book is only for personal use. You cannot amend, distribute, sell, use, quote or paraphrase any part, or the content within this book, without the consent of the author or publisher.

Disclaimer Notice:

Please note the information contained within this document is for educational and entertainment purposes only. All effort has been executed to present accurate, up to date, and reliable, complete information. No warranties of any kind are declared or implied. Readers acknowledge that the author is not engaging in the rendering of legal, financial, medical or professional advice. The content within this book has been derived from various sources. Please consult a licensed professional before attempting any techniques outlined in this book.

By reading this document, the reader agrees that under no circumstances is the author responsible for any losses, direct or indirect, which are incurred as a result of the use of information contained within this document, including, but not limited to, — errors, omissions, or inaccuracies.

Table of Contents

Introduction

Chapter 1 Thinking Logically

Chapter 2 What is Critical Thinking?

Chapter 3 The Winning Skills for Critical Thinking

Chapter 4 The Art of Pattern Recognition and Chunking

Chapter 5 Critical Thinking in Everyday Life

Chapter 6 Critical Thinking Toolbox: Intuitions

Chapter 7 How To Think Logically

Chapter 8 Types of Decision-Making Models

Chapter 9 7 Key Strategies to Improve Problem Solving and Logical Thinking

Chapter 10 The Power of Critical Observation

Chapter 11 Psychology of Arguments

Chapter 12 Basic Argumentation Methods

Chapter 13 Analytical Thinking Exercises to Boost Critical Thinking Skills

Conclusion

Introduction

Do you think you are a decisive person? Well, if you say yes immediately, then you are. However, if your answer is "I don't know," then you probably aren't. Not many people fall into the former category. There are some who are better at decision making than others. Then there are some who can make the RIGHT decision easily when compared to others, and then there are those who need a little help in this department. Regardless of the category that you fall into, decision-making is a skill that comes in handy in every aspect of life. Being able to make right decisions is crucial if you want to succeed in life. Being able to make decisions quickly is equally important. We always have different options and knowing how to select one can have a severe impact on your life.

We go to gatherings to share information, to give an account of undertaking status, to decide, to get the free lunch, and because we were welcomed. (Sorry that I strayed). This is just a halfway rundown - there are numerous other substantial explanations behind holding gatherings.

Maybe the most widely recognized and best purpose behind a gathering, however, is to take care of an issue. A meeting is an excellent spot to do this - you get an assortment of individuals with a variety of encounters, information, and points of view together to guarantee that the ideal arrangement is recognized and that the majority of the significant contemplations have been considered.

The issue is, that while the setting and the general population may be right, frequently the procedure is imperfect. It is defective because one inquiry hasn't been posted and replied.

The concept of critical thinking is foreign to most people, and you are to be congratulated right from the beginning for taking the initiative to learn more about it. You are about to embark on a journey into the thinking process that the majority of the people in the world will never take.

Most people are ignorant of how to think critically because it is generally not taught in schools, which means that most people are not aware of the benefits of critical thought. There are many reasons why there is a lack of emphasis on the teaching of critical thought, but the primary reason is that those who are in charge know that if people actually learned how to skillfully dissect arguments and think critically about all topics, including what our governments and our media sources are feeding us, people would question a lot more of what they are fed by governmental and media institutions and take a lot less of it at face value.

Four Goals for Critical Thinking

An adept critical thinker learns that the process requires a commitment to four goals each time it is used in order to get the most out of the endeavor. The first goal will be to strive for **self-direction**.

Self-directed learning involves taking responsibility for your own acquisition and analysis of factual information from which you will learn. Your decision to dig deeper into ideas requires you to step out of your comfort zone, and you are going to have to make a decision about whether becoming a critical thinker is worth it to you. It is much easier to take things at face value – advertisers, marketers, politicians, and many others prefer that you not become a critical thinker, in fact! Most people are quite comfortable following cues from their highly conditioned subconscious mind and going about their days living in a world where they roll right along with the status quo and, quite frankly, lead mediocre lives. Please understand that this is not a judgmental statement – it is simply a fact. Those who practice self-directed learning do so because they realize that taking issues at face value without questioning the data or the process risk missing the truth behind those issues. Self-directed critical thinkers consciously make a decision to adhere to and follow the principles of critical thought because they see the value in doing so. There is a very good chance that you may be looked down upon by others if you suggest that they slow things down a bit and make an attempt to examine ideas objectively and from different perspectives. If you are self-directed, you will consciously decide to persevere with your critical thinking not because many other people are doing it (because most are not doing it), but because you realize the value of the practice.

The second goal as a critical thinker is do develop a strong sense of **self-discipline**. As stated previously, learning and practicing critical thought is very challenging. Becoming a practicing critical thinker does not happen overnight and must be looked at as a process that takes a lot of introspection, self-analysis, and a commitment to change. And, if you have ever decided to learn a new skill and found it very difficult in the past, it is quite possible that you thought about giving up at some point because you found the work too hard. This is why so many New Year's resolutions are broken every year. As an example, one can visit a fitness center on January 2nd of any given year and usually find it to be very crowded, and visit the same fitness center forty-five days later and see a marked difference in attendance. Self-discipline is not easy.

As you begin to practice critical thinking, particularly in the beginning of your journey, you are going to be tempted to kick back and just continue processing information the way you always did, particularly when your emotions are at play. This makes sense because your subconscious mind has been conditioned to avoid challenges like critical thinking and it will work hard to remind you of your biases, stereotypes, and dysfunctional habits have gotten you this far in life and should not be discarded so flippantly. As a critical thinker, you will use your self-discipline to honestly examine your own biases and habits, and you will push yourself to question your old ways of thought, as well as seek out and evaluate alternative perspectives that you may have never considered before. The good news is that although the work of a new critical thinker can seem overwhelming, it does get easier the more one practices the tenets of critical thinking.

How does one maintain the self-discipline necessary to work through the obstacles to becoming a practicing critical thinker? One does it by using the same techniques one would use to maintain the self-discipline needed to tackle any other challenging endeavor. One of the tricks to maintaining self-discipline is to consciously commit to the process and then write down a statement of that commitment in your own words. As you write, include not only that you are going to work hard to improve your thinking skills, but also include why you are going to learn as much as you can about critical thinking and work to practice it daily. Why are you bothering to put yourself through the work? Most importantly, what do you expect to gain out of it?

Another way to develop and strengthen your self-discipline is to seek out support from others who are learning about critical thinking as you are, or who are critical thinkers at a more advanced stage. Anyone who either understands, or is working to understand, the power of critical thought can be a great resource for you. Share ideas with them, ask questions of them, and share your struggles with them, particularly as you begin learning about critical thinking. You may have to work to find others who define themselves as critical thinkers, but they are not too difficult to find if you know the type of behaviors they typically exhibit.

Critical thinking courses are taught on many college campuses, and there are many websites devoted to the practice through which you may be able to connect with other people committed to the work as well.

The third goal for a critical thinker is **self-monitoring**.

The biases and stereotypes we have taken on in our lives are a direct result of our past experiences and the knowledge we have acquired from those experiences, as well as from what we have learned from those around us, and they may or not be accurate to some degree. Your mission as a critical thinker is to question your preconceived notions about your world and to assess and evaluate their level of accuracy as you move forward with your new ways of thought.

Scientists, for example, conduct experiments based on a theory they have about how a change in one variable may change another. More often than not, they have an idea about how those variables will interact with one another before they conduct the experiment, which may affect either the outcome of their experiment or their belief about the outcome of the experiment. Competent and ethically principled scientists are well aware of their biases and try very hard to filter them out of their experiments.

They do this by replicating the experiment several times, and also by sharing their methodology and their data with other scientists for review so that others can check for true scientific validity. As critical thinkers, we have to perform similar operations in order to make sure we have been successful in filtering out our biases. Self-monitoring is a part of that filtering process as we make decisions, set goals, and solve problems. We as critical thinkers have to be careful to self-monitor our thoughts and our actions in order to treat people and ideas objectively as we seek to understand them.

The fourth goal a critical thinker must strive for is one of **self-correction**. This occurs when we reflect upon how we have perceived things in the past and then make decisions about the accuracy of those perceptions. This can be especially difficult because the knowledge base that resides in our subconscious has been hard-wired over the years. In order to have the self-discipline to correct erroneous thinking patterns (see how these goals work together?), we have to see the value of doing so. Critical thinkers will undoubtedly tell you that the benefit is that when you seek out and study various perspectives of issues, there is an opportunity for personal growth. They will also tell you, though, that questioning and correcting inaccurate perceptions that have been held throughout your life may cost you in terms of relationships. Not everyone around you will understand why you are suddenly questioning beliefs that they have held along with you for so long.

Critical thinkers will be more skilled at discussing, articulating, and interpreting the concepts and ideas presenters use to support their arguments. It is quite difficult to make rational decisions based upon learned information if one cannot accurately understand the concepts being discussed. The systems involved in exercising critical thought provide a method of breaking down concepts so that not only it is possible to better understand them, but the ability to discuss and share that understanding with others is enhanced as well.

Chapter 1
Thinking Logically

Have you ever been jealous of those people who seem not to have difficulty solving complex problems you personally find hard to decipher, or those people who can come up with effective decisions at times of peril, and those professionals and executives who have succeeded in their respective careers because of their ability to handling difficult situations?

Most likely, your answer would be yes. It really is intimidating to see your classmate, workmate, or your boss manage their lives efficiently, while you on the other hand, see it all as a jumble and more than once, you have ended up making the wrong decisions and taking the wrong actions in life. These people are called logical thinkers, and an important detail you should know is that most of them were born with the talent of deductive reasoning. It is in their genes. However, it is also worth noting that a percentage of the logical thinkers is actually made up of those who developed their ability to think logically. And so, it is very possible for you to become a logical thinker, too!

Logical Thinking Then and Now

Logical thinking is the process in which we use reasoning consistently to arrive at a conclusion. Problems or situations that require logical thinking call for structure, relationships or connections between facts, and links to reasoning that fits or seems right. The basis of thinking logically is called "sequential thought." This process involves taking ideas, facts, and conclusions that are involved in a problem and then the thinker arranges them in a chain-like manner that takes on a meaning in and of itself. Logical thinking is a step-by-step method.

The history of logical thinking dates back thousands of years. The prominent logical intellects were the Greeks. Greek civilization blessed us with countless contributions of knowledge and wisdom in almost every field including science, philosophy, mathematics, architecture, and politics among others.

Modern history has witnessed a high dependence on the logical approach to thinking. It is the basis on which modern technology, new political theories, discoveries in science, and others are founded. Logical thinking relates to the left side of the brain. Professor Roger Sperry of the University of California, who discovered that different sides of the brain were responsible for different functions, found out that the left-brain deals with functions which are mainly analytical. These functions include dealing with inputs in sequence, seeing the parts of something (e.g. a situation) rather than the whole, and managerial judgments (setting goals, plans, and reviews).

The world of professionals demands logical thinking, especially in the technical jobs like information technology, engineering, business administration, and law. These jobs need people who can diagnose the problems their clients or end users are having. The success in these industries depends on how well these professionals deal with their respective workloads.

The Left Brain

The left side of the brain, which is responsible for logical thinking, takes control when we are working with confirmable and reasonably certain information. This information has been confirmed scientifically. Using verified information allows us to make logical deductions that improve our knowledge. It is the kind of thinking we use in playing board games that have definite rules (chess, for example), and solving puzzles or crosswords which require a specific answer.

SMART Process

Logical thinking is a step-by-step process. The following are the five steps that will help you improve or start thinking logically. These five steps are what make up the SMART process.

First, you need a clear goal or solution. Working towards clear goals or solutions is often characterized by the mnemonic SMART – which stands for goals that are Specific, Measurable, Achievable, Realistic, and Time-bounded. Using this process to meet goals provides a broader definition on what you are trying to do that will help you succeed.

Systematic planning is the second step of the SMART process towards achieving our goal. Whereas the SMART method has defined our goals, systematic planning helps us know "how" the goals will be achieved. Systematic planning aims to find the 3 corrects (correct method, the correct procedure, and the correct system) that can take us to our goal by using logic.

Using the left side of our brains to work towards our goals are basically what the remaining steps in the SMART process are all about. In this phase of the process, information is the main tool. After information is grouped, it is organized, ranked, fit it into the bigger picture, and then links are created between details to find connections and relationships between them.

Reasoning is the fourth step of the SMART process after the information is analyzed. By using the faculties of our mind for reasoning, we compare things presented as perceptions or concepts, resulting in taking in the new amount of thoughts, and then weaving them all into a more difficult and elaborate kind of mental fabric that we often call abstract, or sometimes general ideas in the truth. This is a critical stage in logical thinking, since how we analyze the information through reasoning sets the stage for how our conclusion, solution, or decision will be formulated to the relevant situation.

Formulated conclusions are the products of the scientific and logical approach of thinking and seeing things. Before conclusions are transformed into decisions and then actions, they should be double, or tripled checked for errors. We need to see whether we really have come up with the best solution to the problem before executing it, or whether the conclusion we have is the truth or not. If the information is processed thoroughly throughout the SMART process, the conclusions are usually the workable solutions that are needed in the situations the thinker or his environment encounters.

Although it may sound like an exhausting process, SMART is actually an easy one if only applied from time to time. If we use this daily, then conflicts can be avoided and prejudices can to be stopped.

Improving Your Logical Thinking Ability

There are many ways to improve your newfound ability in logical thinking. Don't worry, these do not include reading philosophy books, or law codes (although it would certainly be awesome if you do). The following tips aim at developing your logical thinking skills while having fun at the same time.

Crossword puzzles and solving complex sudokus are remarkable mind boosters. Filling in crosswords makes you scan your brain for specific areas of your memory to locate specific information or facts that will lead you to the right answer, while sudokus lets you utilize your analytical and mathematical skills. This type of mind booster is terrific food for your brain that will certainly speed up the development of your logic skills.

Recent studies from prominent universities such as Harvard indicated that exercise and classical music induce our mind to have improved memory and better thinking. Socializing is also a plus since meeting other people lets us learn new ideas, and also allows us to let our minds exercise logical thinking during conversations with other people. Like conversations in social circles, joining or engaging in a debate is also mind boosting, only more rigorous. Debates require our logical skills to be optimized since by thinking logically, you refute whatever your opponent tries to prove.

Logical thinking helps you distinguish the truth from the lies, solve complex problems, and make workable decisions – just make sure to implement the SMART process in order to make sure the information your logic stands on is reliable and significant enough. Because of today's technological advancements, information is available almost everywhere, and so it is important to know that not all of this information is true or reliable. You have to rely on your own brain and know what's wrong or right. Logical thinking is what gives you the power to separate the facts from the hoaxes; and the good thing is you don't have to possess genes for that, you just have to make it a priority and practice it whenever possible. Happy thinking!

The Critical Thinker's Toolkit

How do you normally make decisions? Do you have a particular strategy you like to follow? Every day we are called upon to make choices, big ones, inconsequential ones; occasionally the life or death kind. Big or small, there's no escaping them. Oh, to be sure, they may not always be life-altering, but we can't away from them.

From the time you wake up in the morning, which is, by the way, a decision you make, to the time you fall asleep you are making choice after choice, even if you aren't aware that you are.

Even NOT making a decision is making a decision, right? You put off or postpone a decision, perhaps, but that still is making a choice. Most of us struggle to some degree with decision-making, even though we're making them several times a day. At some point, you'd think we would get better at making them just because we've had so much experience. But here's the rub. Just because we have to make decisions constantly doesn't mean we've gotten very good at making them or that we make them as easily as we could. We've all had a lot of practice with decision-making strategies that don't work all that well. Some work better than others. Here are some ways you may make decisions now. See if any of these strategies look familiar:

Trial and Error

We could also call this the "let's just see" method. When we aren't sure what's the best course of action to take we experiment with one choice or another and see how that works out for us.

Go with Your Gut

While we're not sure how or when it works, we can try to choose our next course of action based on what our instincts are telling us. How reliable are the knots in your stomach and just what exactly is your sixth sense trying to tell you?

Worry

Have you ever lost a night's sleep running your problem around in your head on some kind of endless loop? Do you run different scenarios over and over in your head, asking yourself, what if? What if? What if? We can spend so much time and energy fretting over our situation we literally make ourselves sick and still we don't come up with a good solution.

Seek Counsel

do you ask an expert, a trusted friend, a higher power? Do you trust other people and their opinions over your own? How has that worked out in the past?

Bury Your Head in the Sand

When all else fails, we can morph into ostriches, and just pretend the problem doesn't exist. Funny isn't it? When we emerge from wherever we've had our heads buried, the problem is usually right there.

Act First and Ask Questions Later

Or are you an-any-action-is-better-than-no-action kind of person? Are your watchwords: "Fire, ready, aim!"

A Better Way

All of those strategies are what we could call "hit or miss" propositions. Any one of those strategies would probably work in your favor on occasion. Like that old expression says, even a blind squirrel can dig up an acorn once in a while.

Still, since we do have to make decisions every day of our lives, wouldn't it be a good idea if we got better at doing so? And wouldn't it be great if we could make them in half the time?

Doesn't it make sense that we should find a tried and true system we could use to make any kind of decision but especially with the ones that are most significant?

You probably have a "system" you use to get yourself ready every morning to face the day. Maybe you layout your clothes the night before and set the timer on the coffee maker before you go to bed. By performing the same tasks the same way, you can get ready quickly and efficiently. You organize your different steps in a way that makes it easy – bathe, dress, breakfast.

That's the secret behind using critical thinking to make good decisions – the right system. All you need to make excellent well-founded decisions for the rest of your life is a handful of critical thinking skills, included in your critical thinking tool kit, these are your identification, study, examination, evaluation and decision tools.

Chapter 2
What is Critical Thinking?

What was the hardest decision you ever had to make?

Was it picking out a college? Choosing a career? Deciding where to live?

Every day we have to make all kinds of decisions, some are inconsequential and some are hugely important with serious consequences. Sometimes, making a choice is relatively easy, and other times in can be an anguishing experience.

Doesn't it seem like some people just seem to have an easier time deciding what to do in a situation than others? It's almost like they have an extra-special "decider" gene in their DNA.

How to you customarily make your decisions? Is it easy for you to decide what to do? Are some choices easier than others?

It only makes sense that decisions are only as good as the thought we put into them. If we can think better, we can make better decisions. So, let's learn how to think better. But first, let's head for the pool.

Swimming Pools and Brains

Imagine you were going to go swimming at the local pool. It's a regular, Olympic sized, regulation pool with a deep end and a shallow end, steps on both sides.

If you wanted, you could tiptoe down the steps in the shallow end, just deep enough to get wet, splash around a bit, and then get right out. Technically, since you moved your body through the water, you were, sort of, swimming.

But you didn't get all of the experience that you could, did you? You didn't use as much of the swimming pool as you might have.

You could have waded in a little bit, and used a little more of what the swimming pool had to offer.

Or, if you had the right skills and knew some different strokes, you might have floated a while and then propelled yourself all the way across the length of the pool, from the shallow end to the deep end. Then, using different abilities, you might plunge below the surface, all the way down to the bottom of the pool. Whoohoo! Then you'd really be swimming!

We could even say you were "critically" swimming, because you used several different strokes and skills to swim: wading, floating, diving, crawling, backstroking, holding your breath, synchronizing your hand and arm movements, regulating your breathing. You get the picture.

It didn't take a lot of skill to get down the steps and into the water and stand up in the shallow end with water up to your neck. That was pretty automatic.

It took more skill to wade out a little bit and bob up and down and keep your head above water. It took more to float and dog paddle, and more to swim deftly using special strokes.

That's the difference between swimming and critically swimming. The amount of skills involved and how fully you experience everything the pool has to offer.

That's exactly how critical thinking differs from plain old garden-variety thinking. Regular thinking is pretty automatic. Critical thinking takes some skill. You need to learn some different strokes to get the most out of swimming and you need to learn some different techniques to get the most out of thinking.

A critical swimmer would use a particular stroke for maximum effect. They may be called different things, the Australian crawl or the breaststroke, but they are designed to get you from one end of the pool to the other.

Critical thinkers think using the best tools they have. Some of those jargon-filled buzz words you no doubt stumbled over reading about critical thinking? They are just different names for different tools in the Critical Thinker's tool box. While they may be called different things and expressed different ways, there are basically five tools you need to use to get you from one end of the decision-making process to the other. You will most often use them in order, one after the other, but there will be times you will go back and use some of them more than once.

When you go to a pool, you can choose to use all of it to the best of your ability, employing various. When you go to use your brain, you can choose to use it a little or a lot. You can think or think deeply. When you have to make a decision, you can shoot from the hip, off the top of your head, not think about it very much at all, cross your finger and hope for the best, or you can think about what you're thinking about and achieve the best possible outcome.

Characteristics of Critical Thinkers

Critical Thinkers strive to be Ethical and Fair

There are plenty of very strong thinkers in the world who are experts at using their thinking skills to get what they want at the expense of others. Unscrupulous lawyers and accountants, for example, are highly skilled at looking at situations and then building solid arguments to support the best interests of their clients, while not even considering what is true or what is ethical. Using ethics and fairness as critical thinking skills are applied will allow the practitioner to not only elevate himself as he seeks to solve problems, but will also allow him to be a strong role model for others who aspire to develop skills associated with critical thought.

Ethical and fair critical thinkers analyze and assess their own thinking as carefully as they analyze and assess the thinking and reasoning of others. Introspective reflection can be defined as thinking about the way one uses his own mind to think. When we evaluate our own thought processes, we are looking to see how our own biases may be affecting our perspectives. In addition, we are examining how our emotions may be getting in the way of making sound decisions that could move us forward with more focus and with potentially better outcomes.

Critical Thinkers Are Open-Minded

Do you have friends or acquaintances who always have to be right and have a very difficult time admitting when they are wrong? Chances are pretty good that they are not critical thinkers. Sound critical thinking requires vulnerability that allows the thinker not only to be aware of other peoples' biases, but to develop an awareness of their own biases as well. A humble critical thinker realizes that his own paradigms of looking the world around him may in fact be flawed in some way.

Humility in thinking is a challenging virtue to achieve for many people, because we have often grown up with prejudices and biases that have been passed to us through teachers, parents, our cultures, our social groups, our friends, and the institutions with which we have had associations. We may strongly believe, for example, that our own religion is the only one that is true, and we may never even take the time or expend the energy to study and learn about other religions. Our "intellectual arrogance" is an obstacle to opening our minds to the possibility that other religions may have validity as well.

Open-minded critical thinkers are willing to consider other perspectives within any given issue, knowing that even if they do not end up agreeing with the other perspective, at least they have given themselves the opportunity to learn about how others think or feel about the given issue. This knowledge expands the critical thinker's knowledge base, which can only enhance his understanding about the world around him and the people who live in it.

Critical Thinkers Possess Mental and Emotional Fortitude

Mental and emotional fortitude come into play when we become critical thinkers because it's not easy to begin to question beliefs we have held our entire lives. It may seem much easier to avoid the work in front of us, which includes examining our own patterns of thought and behavior and considering what is true and what is not based upon the evidence we find. What will it mean if you come to the conclusion that a strong belief you have had since childhood turns out to be false? How will you handle that new information, and what will it mean to have to adjust your life accordingly? One has to possess courage in order to do the work required of a critical thinker because of what one may discover about past beliefs.

A critical thinker also has to be courageous because they may be viewed as a nonconformist in the eyes of their peers. One of the most important points you will learn as you continue working through this book is that critical thinking is not all that common in our society, which can serve to make it a lonely endeavor. The concepts of critical thinking are not really taught to us in our schools or in our homes. There are many reasons for this which are discussed in other parts of this book, but the point being made here is that because most people are not critical thinkers, your friends and your family may not really understand you when you begin to question the concepts you have held close your entire life. Even if your views remain the same, your new way of assessing, evaluating, and reflecting may seem so foreign to your coworkers and your loved ones that they may reject you in some way or fashion. As a critical thinker, you are going to have to figure out how you will respond to their questions and possible rejection. Hopefully, you will take the time to show them this book and get them started on their own path to being strong-minded critical thinkers.

Critical Thinkers Have Empathy for Diverse Perspectives

Many people confuse empathy with sympathy, but they are not the same thing. Whereas sympathy is feeling bad or sad for someone, empathy is being able to understand something from someone else's perspective. Some have described empathy as the ability to be able to stand in another person's shoes. Empathy is a learned skill and while many people are aware of the concept, fewer practice it regularly. Why? Because it is easier to see things from our own perspective and it is challenging to consider the perceptions of others.

A good illustration of empathy is how different people perceive those who are addicted to drugs or alcohol. On one hand, a large part of society tends to view addicts as weak-willed people who consciously choose to engage in their addictive behavior and could quite easily change their lives if they just decided to do it. This group tends to judge addicts harshly and often advocates jail or prison time for drug offenses.

Conversely, another segment of society, which includes many people who work with addicts, seeks to learn about the reasons behind the user's addictive behavior. These people seek to understand the factors that led the person to use their addictive substance in the first place, as well as the factors that get in the way of the addict being able to recover from his addiction.

One cannot fully develop as a strong critical thinker until he decides to actively seek to understand other perspectives on any issue he is examining. It is not enough to simply examine the surface level of other perspectives; instead, one must examine the evidence and facts that others use to support the perspectives they support. All too often, people dismiss other peoples' opinions or beliefs on issues by dismissing them without trying to understand why others feel the way that they do. While a critical thinker may not agree with another view after fully examining it, he will at least gain a deeper understanding of other views on issues from studying them.

Critical Thinkers Possess Determination

You will read throughout this book that thinking critically is not always easy, particularly in the beginning when the concepts involved in critical thinking are new to you. The other fact that makes critical thinking a challenge is that not many people are aware of what it means to be a critical thinker, and thus do not practice it. Just like any other new skill you may learn in your life, critical thought takes a lot of practice to become skilled at it, and you will hit your roadblocks. When you get stuck, or feel like slipping into your old ways of thinking, you must get in touch with why you took up the study of critical thinking in the first place and reconnect with your motivation. Those who become practicing critical thinkers reap benefits that the rest of the world do not realize.

Critical Thinkers Possess Intellectual Freedom

One of the most important qualities that a critical thinker enjoys is the autonomy to think for himself. People who do not learn to think critically often have their opinions and ideas shaped by others, or are so bound by their biases that they shun the opinions of others. Strong thinkers who learn to apply the concepts of critical thought in their lives realize that they have the freedom to think for themselves and make their own decisions independent of influences like past bias, the media, the government, or others around them. Intellectual freedom is powerful because it helps the critical thinker find the truth, or at least develop an opinion that has been made by systematically researching all perspectives.

Critical Thinkers Have Self-Confidence

Once you begin to work with your new critical thinking skills, you will develop confidence in your thinking processes because you will know that they are systematic and sound. This does not mean that all of your problem-solving from this point forward will be easy, because you will still have to wrestle with your emotions if they conflict with your logic in terms of making a particular decision. However, if you use your critical thinking skills to help solve your problems or to answer important questions that you must ask, you will have the confidence and satisfaction knowing that you have considered all of the options available to you in a systematic and thorough way.

Chapter 3
The Winning Skills for Critical Thinking

Interpretation

This not only includes the ability to understand the information that you have been presented with but also includes your ability to be able to communicate its meaning to others. You will find yourself in different situations where you will need to make use of this critical skill. Interpretational skills will help you in getting a better understanding of the information that you have been presented with, and it also helps in decoding the same. Doing this will provide you some clarity. Application exercise: Make a list of 10 facial expressions that can be equated to different emotions. For instance, a smile means happiness; a frown can mean confusion and so on. Try analyzing the different emotions you can gauge by looking at someone else's expressions.

Information Seeking

Critical thinking is about taking the facts and combining them with what you know to create perspective. This perspective helps you decide based on what you have learned and any other factors that come into play. The importance of logic in critical thinking makes information seeking a big part of the critical thinking process. This is especially true since the knowledge that you have affects your perspective, as well as the variety of the options available to you.

Application exercise: Imagine that your boss comes to you with a big project—working with the budgeting department to implement an energy-saving plan for the company. The goal is to maximize the benefits while spending as little on equipment and energy-saving alternatives as possible.

As the field of energy technology is rapidly expanding, this is something that you will want to research before diving into it. Carry out research and come up with an energy-saving plan that is effective, but cost-friendly.

Stimulating Thinking

There are opportunities all around you that you can use to practice critical thinking through your day. For example, when your coworker asks you to complete their assignment over the weekend, you have to critically think about it. Consider if you would be sacrificing something, like plans you had previously made. Then, think about the coworker and if there are any benefits. There are times when you can (and should) help others without expecting anything back, but it should not be a one-sided relationship. Be kind, but do not be afraid to say no, whether you had plans or just wanted to relax over the weekend. Answering them should not be an instantaneous response—take the time to critically think. By taking advantage of situations like these, you are getting the practice you need to become 'good' at critical thinking.

Application exercise: One of the easiest ways to stimulate critical thinking is by asking yourself questions about a scenario. Ask things like, 'What is my point of view on this topic?' and 'Why do I believe that?' Answer these questions and identify your reasoning for your point of view and consider any alternative perspectives that might exist. This process can be applied to any scenario in your life to create a critical thinking situation.

Analysis

Being able to connect the different pieces of information that you have been provided with and determining the intended meaning of the same is known as analysis. This skill lends its user the ability to read between the lines and will help you in understanding the actual meaning of something. Analysis is an easy skill to acquire, but it does take a while to master.

Application exercise: If you are interested in starting to practice this skill, then try to understand the meaning of this Chinese proverb "Be the first to the field and the last to the couch." Did you understand what this proverb is trying to convey? We will obviously all have a different interpretation, but this proverb is essentially talking about hard work.

Non-Judgment

It is essential for critical thinkers to view different perspectives without being judgmental. Critical thinking requires you to consider different viewpoints in a way that is objective, taking in the knowledge without emotionally charging it or manipulating it to fit your agenda. It is easy to let emotions cloud judgment, especially when you are passionate about your topic. However, if you let bias cloud your view, then you can never be sure if the conclusion you have drawn comes from the facts or the emotions in the situation.

Application exercise: Practicing mindfulness helps you learn how to acknowledge your thoughts without letting them cloud your judgment. Start by bringing your mind to a state of focus and relaxation. Sit in a quiet room and take some deep breaths, paying attention to the feeling of your belly falling and rising. Once you feel relaxed, open your eyes and choose a point of focus. You can watch a beetle on the windowsill, observe the wood patterns on your desk, or look at a painting on the wall. Look at your chosen point of focus and observe it without analyzing it or judging it in any way. If you do think something, observe the thought without becoming emotionally attached to it. Focus on your breaths again until your mind clears and return to your main point of focus.

Inference

The ability to conclude by understanding and recognizing the different elements that you are presented with is known as inference. Well, most people tend to jump to a conclusion without taking into consideration all the information that is available. Doing this will lead to faulty assumptions and, in turn, it can affect your ability to take decisions. Think of a scenario where you are the business manager, and you are looking at the sales forecast. You notice that the sales have dropped. It is essential that you can take into consideration other additional information to determine the exact reason for the decrease in sales. There can be internal and external issues that led to the decline in the sales.

Application exercise: Select a crime show and watch one episode per week. Notice and observe the different clues that they drop and see if you can figure out on your own who the culprit is, before the end of the show. This will help you with your inferential skills.

Evaluation

This refers to the skill of being able to evaluate the credibility of a statement or the information that you have been presented. This skill comes in handy when you have measured the validity of the information on hand.

Application exercise: There is a very easy way in which you can hone this skill. Just open your laptop and search for tests for evaluation skills and voila! You will have plenty of tests to choose from, and this will help you in developing your evaluation skills.

Explanation

Explanation is the skill of being able to restate the information in such a way that it adds clarity and perspective to it. This is needed so that such information can be adequately understood. For instance, think of a scenario where you have to give two presentations about a new product idea - one for the board of directors of the company and other to the product engineers. Both the parties will be keen on listening to what you have to say. However, the way you present the information before these two groups will be significantly different. The board will probably be interested in only the high-level idea whereas the team of product engineers will be interested in learning about the specific details of the product. Your ability to explain your idea while taking into consideration the audience you are presenting to is quintessential to make sure that the information is not just well received but is understood as well.

Application exercise: A really simple way in which you can hone this skill is by explaining a rather complicated concept to two different people. You can use your kids and your spouse for this. The way you explain a particular concept to your spouse will be different from the way in which you will explain it to your children. The goal is quite simple - the audience should understand what you are saying.

Communication

One commonly overlooked skill in the art of critical thinking is communication. Even the most intelligent, introverted individuals have to communicate to be successful at critical thinking.

Communication is useful in many stages of the critical thinking process. During the information seeking stage, you might need to speak to or communicate with others to ask about research they have done or their knowledge on the subject you are studying. Communicating with others can also help you learn about other perspectives or ideas that are relevant, which is important for coming up with alternative choices. Even after you have finished researching your ideas, it is important to use communication to share what you have learned. This is true whether your idea was a success or not—sharing gives everyone the opportunity to learn from your thoughts and ideas.

Application exercise: Next time you critically think about an idea, take the time to thoroughly research it and come up with different perspectives. Use what you have learned to create a PowerPoint presentation, as if you were going to give a slideshow presentation and explain the idea and different perspectives that exist.

Creativity

Some people overlook creativity as an important trait, especially for something like critical thinking that focuses on logical thought. Even so, critical thinking requires creativity when coming up with alternatives and problem solving. It is essential and as simple as knowing when to step outside of the box and come up with an unconventional solution. Being creative broadens your perspective and gives you greater insight into the possibilities of the world.

Have you ever noticed that children are more likely to be in touch with their imagination than adults? As we age, we are often told that we should focus on logic and completing our studies. This can be beneficial to intelligence—but intelligence is worth nothing unless you have the ability and creativity that are necessary to use it.

Over time, focusing our brains away from the creative side of things causes our mind to disregard creative ideas before we consciously have them. This means that even though our minds are still capable of creative thought, we are not receiving the ideas in our conscious mind. It is like a phone call going through to a line with no service—the connection to that creative thought cannot be completed.

Application exercise: Fostering creativity in your life is as simple as getting in the habit of trying new things. Take a dance class or order something new at a restaurant. Creative thought can also be benefited through creative acts, like sewing, crafting, painting, writing, playing a musical instrument, singing, or any other number of activities.

Self-Regulation

This refers to having an awareness of your thinking process and the elements that you make use of for finding the results that you did. Self-regulation is important because it helps you avoid bias in your thinking. For example, imagine that you are trying to convince one of your parents to try a new pharmaceutical drug that can help treat their heart disease. If you are trying to convince them to take the medicine, you might look up the positives for the drug and fail to look up the possible side effects. This gives you a limited view and makes your thinking process (and the conclusions you draw) invalid.

Application exercise: Imagine that you are on a call with a customer and are trying to help the customer fix a problem with the company's software that they are using. Also, this is your first week at the job. The problem that you are trying to rectify is a difficult one, but you want to assist the customer in making a good impression. Well, the ideal thing to do is to transfer that call to a coworker with prior experience in the same, and this will help the customer obtain the best results. This is about learning to differentiate between your personal biases while making a decision related to your work. Don't let your self-interests hinder your ability to decide what is best for your work.

Using Reason

At the foundation of critical thinking is reasoning. Even if you are making a decision that involves emotion, you must keep your thinking rational and reasonable. For example, a person may stay in a relationship based on the rationale that the other person loves them or needs them. It is even possible they have grown to love the other person, even though they are abusive. In this case, emotional thinking is harmful because within any rational thought, the only logical solution is to leave the relationship.

Reasoning involves using rational, factual pieces of information to reach your conclusion. It involves using the logical side of the brain rather than the emotional and basing your conclusions on knowledge instead of feelings. This gives you the goal of thinking clearly and making sounder decisions.

Application exercise: Envision a scenario where someone you are close to, like a sibling, friend, or significant other, comes to you with a problem. The problem is illegal, unethical, or otherwise undesirable to be in.

Think of different scenarios that result from this incident. For example, if someone close to you says that they killed someone, some potential outcomes would be trying to cover it up or calling the police to report the scenario.

Think of factors that might lead to each of these decisions. For example, how the person was killed. Then, imagine the results and how it would affect everyone involved. Think about the way that logic and emotion affected the decision in each of the scenarios.

Reevaluation

Critical thinkers understand that knowledge is not absolute. Technology is constantly advancing, and the field of science is researching and pushing further each day to give us a deeper and greater understanding of the world around us.

As new information becomes available, it is important to reevaluate what you know and what you have learned. Look at new information objectively, to determine if decisions you have made, or your viewpoint is going to change.

By keeping current on the decisions that you make that influence your life, you are continuing on the path toward meeting your goals.

Application exercise: Choose a topic that you are passionate about and do research, looking for sources that are at least 10-20 years old. Gather information using these older sources. Then, do a search for newer information on your chosen topic. Evaluate how much the field has changed in just 10-20 years. This showcases how important it is to always stay current with information before making decisions.

Well, these skills can be cultivated quite easily, but if you want to master them, then you will need to put in considerable time and effort for doing the same. This practice will give you the confidence that you need to successfully use these skills in your daily life.

Chapter 4
The Art of Pattern Recognition and Chunking

Apart from doodling, there are also other creative ways for people to improve their memory. As a matter of fact, there are endless ways to enhance a person's memory as there are always endless possibilities open to a creative person. With the help of creativity, we are able to come up with new and relatively exciting ways for us to be able to improve the way we remember and memorize things.

One of these creative memorization techniques is what is known as "pattern recognition." A person's memory, deductive reasoning, recall, and overall mental capacity are said to be excessively improved through our ability to recognize patterns and derive bigger ideas or extrapolate from them.

This concept has made incredible advances in the realm of artificial intelligence possible, but most experts note that it plays a key role as well in enhancing one's own intelligence and even increase one's speed of thought. Simply put, pattern recognition allows us to be able to think faster since we become more adept in analyzing data and making out connections between various objects more quickly.

And there is even better news to this and that is that pattern recognition is actually a very easy skill to develop, only requiring a few simple exercises.

This is because the skills required in pattern recognition are integrated in almost every aspect of our daily lives – gaming, problem solving, decision making, and simply life in general.

The more complicated and more varied the patterns we become exposed to and we are able to recognize, the easier and faster it will be for us to develop new skills and enhance our abilities in pattern recognition. One of the simplest pattern recognition activities that most of us learn in school would be analyzing analogies. Analogies, no matter how simple, require us to find an association or connection between two seemingly different objects and use that connection to solve a given equation.

That same process of pattern recognition enables us to have a keener and better memory. This improvement in our brain capacity might as well be the demarcation line between us and monkeys, as suggested by Daniel Bor. He aimed to shed light on how our inherent ability in pattern recognition can be vital to our conscious awareness and our whole life as well as how it transcends to what makes human being human.

Numerous experiments even prior to Bor have consistently shown that the human brain can hold an average of 4 different things in its working memory. In comparison, monkeys are able to hold 3 or 4. This is where Bor discussed the concept of chunking – the concept which, according to him, makes the difference.

Chunking is described as a kind of "cognitive compression mechanism" in which humans break down huge pieces of information into smaller, more easily remembered chunks. These chunks make the process of memorization a simpler task as it paves way for easy processing of the various information we are exposed to. Bor explains this further by saying that chunking is a little like giving something your attention. You are trying to retain a certain amount of information with your thought processes. You also use preexisting information to make that new information more compact that means it's easier to learn.

To illustrate just how much chunking is of help to our memorization dilemmas, Bor gives us an unbelievable example revolving around a man who was able to use the process of chunking to massively expand his working memory's capacity. The man, with an average IQ and memory capacity, was put in a psychological experiment wherein the researchers would read to him a set of random digits. His task was to simply repeat the digits in the proper order that he heard them. If he is correct, the next set of digits would be one digit longer. But if he were wrong, the next set would be one digit shorter. This seems like a standard memory test at first, but this young man did the experiment for more than two years – about an hour each day for four days each week.

The result of his initial trial was pretty average and then he started getting better at it, remembering around seven digits in the sequence. This was a notable improvement considering most people only reach roughly 4 numbers. Towards the end of the experiment, around 20 or so months since he began, the young man was able to remember and repeat a set of 80 digits. Bor describes the result of the experiment by explaining that if for example, seven people were to tell you their telephone numbers in quick succession, it is likely that at the end of this, he would be able to retain those numbers and make a list of them without making a blunder.

The question, however, remains. How could a person with average intelligence be able to accomplish such an incredible task? Looking at Bor's response, this clearly shows how it is possible.

In the case cited, the man was a track runner. He was accustomed to thinking in numbers in seconds and minutes. For example, if he took 4 minutes and 21 seconds, he would be able to recall 421 easily. Thus, transferring this skill into his working environment, he would be able to remember more numbers. Then by clustering information within this numerical format, he was able to retain more information and up to 80 digits would easily be retained.

Now, how is this any helpful to our lives? Bor emphasizes that chunking is not only meant for us to excel in useless tasks. (Who needs to remember 80 digits anyway, right?) Chunking, as Bor points out, is part of what make us human. Chunking helps memory retention and that's the overall purpose of human consciousness after all.

Chunking also works in even the simplest of tasks. Say you're in your car, in a hurry, no pen and paper in sight, and your mom calls you to make a quick trip to the grocery and buy milk, oil, tomatoes, ham, eggs, and raisins. Problem is, you have no way of remembering all of those without writing them down. What do you do? Simple – and this is a trick that most people already do in their own time. You create an acronym out of the words you have to remember. In this case, you can opt for MOTHER. The letters that will make up the acronym you choose will serve as your chunks. So instead of trying to remember six words, you only have to remember one word (or six letters).

Chunking, however, is more than just about enabling us to recall and memorize things faster and easier. Bor argues that pattern recognition is also one of the best sources of human creativity. Humans, in their attempt to find patterns and connect disparate ideas and objects together, also develop the ability to use whatever pattern they find and make meaning out of it. Bor discusses that the ability to recognize patterns and remember them allows us to view the world with a wider perspective. He consistently suggests that practicing pattern recognition will feed our creativity in ways nothing else can.

In fact, reading this literature made me see that consciousness is part of chunking and that this is valuable because it means that what we retain is clearer and uses already existing criteria set in our minds to recognize new chunks of information more easily.

That's pretty clever and is used by you on a regular basis, whether you are aware of it or not.

Ultimately, we live in a world where looking for patterns and signs within things has become a normal everyday act. Humans use such patterns to be able to make out or understand a blurry concept or even to make ideas more interesting. We use the patterns and the chunks we find to easily establish relationships between various things. Pattern recognition and chunking allows us to exhaust the capabilities of our brains. Simply put, these two concepts enhance our creative thinking by enabling us to search for the most interesting aspects of every dull and boring scenario – something which has become a powerful tool in forcing us to think more and use our imaginations to their fullest extent. Our quest for patterns and chunks in our lives opens up a whole new world of possibilities and wonder.

Chapter 5
Critical Thinking in Everyday Life

We all have great potential within us, but we don't make use of it. Most of it is lying dormant within us, or it is underdeveloped. Any improvement in thinking cannot take place if there is no conscious commitment towards learning. You cannot improve your game in basketball if you don't put in some effort to do so and the same stands true for critical thinking as well. Like any other skill, the effort is essential for its development. As long as you take your thinking for granted, there is no way in which you can unlock your true potential. Development in your thinking process is gradual, and there are several plateaus of learning that you will have to overcome and hard work is a precondition for all of this. You cannot become an excellent thinker by just wanting to become one. You will have to make a conscious decision of changing certain habits, and this will take some time. So, be patient and don't expect any change to occur overnight.

If you are interested in developing the skill of critical thinking, then you need to understand the different changes that one needs to go through in this process.

Stage 1: You are still unaware of the significant problems or pitfalls in your thinking. You aren't a reflective thinker. Most of us are stuck in this stage.

Stage2: You start developing awareness of the problems in your thinking.

Stage 3: You try working on yourself but not regularly.

Stage 4: You realize the need for regular practice.

Stage 5: You start noticing a change in the way you think.

Stage 6: You develop the ability to become insightful in your thinking.

You can progress through these stages by accepting the fact that there are specific problems in the way you think and you start putting in conscious effort to improve yourself.

In this chapter, you will learn about the nine simple strategies that you can follow for developing yourself as a thinker.

Making use of "wasted" time

All human beings tend to waste time; That is, we fail to make productive use of all the time we have at our disposal. Sometimes we flit from one form of diversion to another, without actually enjoying any of them.

At times we get irritated about matters that are clearly beyond our control. At times, we don't plan well, and this causes a butterfly effect of negative consequences that could all have been easily avoided by simple planning. How many times have you been stuck in the rush hour traffic when you could have easily avoided this by leaving an hour earlier? Apart from all the time that we waste doing nothing, we start worrying about unnecessary things.

Sometimes we regret the way we functioned in the past, or we just end up daydreaming about "what could have been" and "what can be," instead of putting in some effort to achieve results. Well, you need to realize that there is no way in which you can get all the lost time again. Instead, try focusing on all the time that you have at your disposal now. One way in which you can develop the habit of critical thinking is to make use of the time that would have normally been "wasted." Instead of spending an hour in front of the TV flipping through channels and getting bored, you can make use of this time or at least a part of it for reflecting on the day you had, the tasks you accomplished, and all that you need to achieve. Spend this time to contemplate your productivity. Here are a couple of questions that you can ask yourself:

When did I do my worst and best thinking today? What was it that I was thinking about all day long? Did I manage to come to a logical conclusion or was it all in vain? Did I indulge in any negative thinking? Did the negative thoughts just create a lot of unnecessary frustration? If I could repeat this day all over again, what would I change? Did I do something that will help me in achieving my goals? Did I accomplish anything that's worth remembering?

Spend some time answering these questions and record your observations. Over a period of time, you will notice that you have a specific pattern of thinking.

Reshaping Your Character

Select an intellectual trait like perseverance, empathy, independence, courage, humility and so on. Once you have selected a feature, try to focus on it for an entire month and cultivate it in yourself. If the trait you have opted for is humility, then start noticing whenever you admit that you are wrong. Notice if you refuse to admit this, even if the evidence points out that you are wrong. Notice when you start becoming defensive when someone tries to point out your mistake or make any corrections to your work. Observe when your arrogance is preventing you from learning something new. Whenever you notice yourself indulging in any form of negative behavior or thinking, squash such thoughts. Start reshaping your character and start incorporating desirable behavioral traits while giving up on the negative ones. You are your worst enemy, and you can prevent your growth unknowingly. So, learn to let go of all things negative.

Dealing with Your Egocentrism

Human beings are inherently egocentric. While thinking about something, we tend to favor ourselves before anyone else subconsciously. Yes, we are biased towards ourselves. In fact, you can notice your egocentric behavior on a daily basis by thinking about the following questions:

What are the circumstances under which you would favor yourself? Do I become irritable or cranky over small things? Did I do or say something that is "irrational" for merely getting my way? Did I try to impose my opinion on others? Did I ever fail to speak my mind about something I feel strongly about and then regret not doing it later on? Once you have identified the egocentric traits, you can start actively working on rationalizing yourself. Whenever you feel like you are egocentric, think what a rational person would say or do in a similar situation and the way in which that compares to what you are doing.

Redefining the Way in Which You See Things

The world that we live in is social as well as private, and every situation is "defined." The manner in which a situation is defined not only determines how you feel, but the way you act, and its implications. However, every situation can be described in multiple ways. This means that you have the power to make yourself happy and your life more fulfilling. This means that all those situations to which you attach a negative meaning can be transformed into something favorable if you want to. This strategy is about finding something positive in everything that you would have considered to be negative. Try to see the silver lining in every aspect of your life. It is all about perspectives and perceptions. If you think that something is positive, then you will feel good about it, and if you think it's negative, then you will naturally harbor negative feelings towards it.

Get in Touch with Your Emotions

Whenever you start feeling some negative emotion, ask yourself the following:

What line of thinking has led to this emotion? For instance, if you are angry, then ask yourself, what were you thinking about that has caused the anger you are feeling? What are the other ways in which I can view this situation? Every situation seems different depending on your perspective. A negative aspect makes everything seem dull and bleak, and on the other hand, a positive outlook does brighten things up. Whenever you feel a negative emotion creeping up, try to see some humor in it or rationalize it. Concentrate on the thought process that produced the negative emotion, and you can find a solution to your problem.

Analyzing the Influence of a Group on Your Life

Carefully observe the way your behavior is influenced by the group you are in. For instance, any group would have specific unwritten rules of conduct that all the members follow. There will be some form of conformity that will be enforced. Check for yourself how much this influences you and the manner in which it impacts you. Check if you are bowing too much to the pressure that is being exerted and if you are doing something just because others expect it of you.

You don't have to start practicing all the steps at once. Start out slowly and try following as many as you can. Initially, you will need to put in the conscious effort for critical thinking and, over a period, these skills will come naturally to you.

Critical Thinking and Leadership

One might assume that our leaders in government, in business, and in the nonprofit sector are strong critical thinkers. Sadly, this assumption is largely incorrect. While many leaders have at least some of the qualities of critical thinkers, few possess all of them. However, if one aspires to attain a leadership position at some point, or if one is already a leader within a field and desire to improve leadership skills, one could benefit significantly from studying and applying critical thinking skills in his life.

One of the most important characteristics of a successful leader is the he is constantly striving to learn more about himself and to seek self-improvement. Leaders work hard to look within, or, in other words, to do the introspective work as one of the most important tasks of a critical thinker. Leaders must know their strengths and their weaknesses so that they can capitalize on what they do well and work to correct areas in which they fall short. Leaders, like critical thinkers, understand that introspection and reflection are life-long processes that must be done routinely and honestly in order to keep oneself sharp.

The second skill a leader must have is that he must be proficient using the tools and the skill sets that he has. In other words, a strong leader must know how to get things done on a daily basis, using the skills he has acquired throughout his life and his training, as well as the tools available to him, technical and otherwise. Leaders, like critical thinkers, must know what they need in order to get the job done. And, just as important, they must know where to look to get what they need in order to accomplish that specific mission. Like critical thinkers, leaders are not afraid to consider various perspectives in order to solve the often-complex problems that they must address. They will seek out others' opinions, and then take the necessary time to examine the quality of each perspective, taking the time to separate the facts from the opinions. Then, and only then, are leaders able to put themselves in a much stronger position to begin to tactfully prepare a strategy to solve the problem.

The third principle of a strong leader requires leaders to develop a sense of responsibility among subordinates. Leaders engaged in the process of critical thought understand that team-building is a very important function of leadership and the best way to accomplish that goal is by working to instill a sense of comradery among those being led.

This is accomplished by understanding the mission of the team as well as taking the time to learn the individual strengths of each team member and what they can contribute to the team. Then, the leader must facilitate communications among team members that focuses on information-sharing and breaking down the barriers to honest communication.

A fourth principle is that leaders must be able to make sound decisions in a timely manner. This is without a doubt one of the most important tasks in leadership. As we have learned while studying the decision-making process in our examination of critical thought processes, making a decision begins with a clear and precise statement of the problem. Then, leaders must figure out how and where to gather the information that is necessary in order to begin to think about possible solutions to the problem. Once the information has been collected, leaders must separate the facts from the perspectives and carefully consider each piece of data based upon its own merits. Once the evidence has been evaluated, then the leader must construct possible solutions and consider the likely consequences, or implications, of each possibility. Then, the leader is able to move forward with a decision and take action. This is the same process taken by practicing critical thinkers as they approach problems.

Timely decisions are important because leaders are often called upon to make difficult decisions within a very short amount of time. Even when time is short, it is important for leaders, and for critical thinkers, to make every effort to keep their mission in perspective and work as quickly as possible while working to minimize the possibility of compromising the fundamentals of sound decision-making.

A fifth principle of leadership requires leaders to always focus on setting a positive example. Leaders and critical thinkers best set examples by role-modeling examples of integrity and discipline. Leaders who practice the principles of critical thought are in an optimal position to positively affect those whom they lead because through example, they have the opportunity to motivate people to be both strong critical thinkers AND strong leaders! Leaders set examples by behaving in ways that they wish their subordinates to behave, and they are wise to remember that their position as leaders carries with it an awesome responsibility to teach, as well as to lead.

A sixth principle of leadership requires leaders to know the people they are leading and to look out for their welfare, which aligns with the concept of empathy. Leaders are at least in part responsible for those they lead. That role of responsibility may certainly be enhanced in a military environment, for example, but all leaders are at least in part responsible for educating, training, or assisting their subordinates get from Point A to Point B in some fashion. A strong leader seeks to understand those he leads from their perspective as much as that is possible and he works to accomplish that by holding individual or group meetings with them and by actively listening to what they are saying. Contrary to popular belief, a leader is not the only person doing the talking. Instead, good leaders understand that in order to understand the perspectives of their subordinates, they have to ask open-ended questions and then pay close attention to the responses.

A seventh principle of leadership reminds leaders to keep their people informed. Effective communication is absolutely critical in leadership roles and leaders must make sure that the messages they impart to their crews are clear and precise with minimal or no use of vague or ambiguous terms or phrases. Communications should be delivered in a timely manner. When preparing communications, it is important for the leader to consider his biases that may influence what he says or how he says it. He also needs to consider possible biases held by his team members and how those biases may influence their interpretations of the message he is presenting.

An eighth principle of leadership advises leaders to seek responsibility and to take responsibility for one's actions. In terms of critical thinking, this principle addresses the goal of self-direction and self-accountability. Leaders and critical thinkers are charged with offering their talents and their skill sets when they believe it is appropriate to do so, and they don't wait to be spoon-fed information when they need to solve a problem. They find out where to look and then they gather and analyze the data in a timely fashion. They also take responsibility for their shortcomings as well as their successes.

A ninth principle of leadership requires those who lead to make sure that their assigned tasks are understood and that members of their teams get the supervision they need in order to accomplish tasks successfully. This principle addresses the need for clear and precise communication and the need to understand the perspectives of the people charged with getting the job done.

Chapter 6
Critical Thinking Toolbox: Intuitions

Intuition Defined

This is a phenomenon that happens in the mind described as the ability to gain knowledge without the use of reasoning and inference. This is also known as a gut feeling. This came from a Latin word intueri which will be literally translated as consider; or may also be connected to a late Middle English word intuit which is translated as to contemplate. It is considered as an inner perception or real lucidity or understanding. This phenomenon gives understanding, view, belief and judgment which cannot be verified or justified rationally. This phenomenon is a hot topic in psychology, as well as within esoteric and religious domains, and is also included in subjects of writings.

The part of the brain responsible for this phenomenon is the right brain, which is associated with general creative abilities and aesthetic. However, some researchers contented that this is not a creative process, but an innovation of scientific breakthroughs.

Intuition and Decision-Making

The connection of decision- making and intuition is that, it creates a non- sequential information- processing mode. This process is different from insight and can be taken in contrast with the deliberate style of decision making. Intuition has an emotional or cognitive impact on the process of judgement. It may also bridge two individual and make deliberate decision making styles interchangeably. However, there is still no concrete evidence regarding the confirmation of the relationship between intuition and decision making.

How Do Intuition Works?

Intuition works as an advanced pattern recognition device. The subconscious mind tries to find a connection between various patterns from one's past experience and the current situation that this certain individual is facing. Some details of the past cannot be recalled from experience. However, even if you can recall most of the details, it will be hard to express the lessons learned in an applicable, analytical way of reasoning. The subconscious mind can still recall the patterns of your past experience. This makes it easy to project the lessons to be applied to the current situation. The message of wisdom comes from your inner voice and will be expressed in the language of your feelings.

Mental Intuition

There are several forms of intuition. Some clearly observable way of intuition is the mental, emotional, physical and spiritual intuition.

Mental Intuitive Person

A mental intuitive person processes the world through the use of the most powerful part of the body, the mind. There is an inborn desire to gain learning and understand life, spirit and humanity in general. They experience the: need of seeking the truth above all else; firm desire of knowing, learning and expanding minds; absorption of possibility and truth; and the capacity to intuit patterns and logic and sum up those parts.

The Influence of a Mental Intuitive to the Persons Around Him

A mental intuitive person can: provide insight on how to solve certain problems; push other people to explore alternatives on how to find a solution on global and local issues; and create promises and hopes for other people.

Side Effects of Being a Mental Intuitive

Because the mind of a mental, intuitive requires so much energy in processing, their thoughts might overwhelm them. Unrealistic expectations can be formed regarding things which can be accomplished and put pressure on themselves. Physical ailments may manifest headaches, insomnia, muscle tension and stress, sinus issues and panic or anxiety.

Staying Healthy and Well Balanced- Mental Intuitive

A mental intuitive needs ample time to quite their mind and meditation is not appropriate. They only need time to sit in a quite place. They also need physical activity to break the stress of too much churning of the mind. They also need to open up themselves for the assurance and love from partner, family and friends. A mental intuitive has a high tendency of feeling undervalued and get wrapped up to their way of thinking, giving them the feeling of forgetting the real world around them.

How to Make the Most Out of Being a Mental Intuitive

Being a mental intuitive means having the gift of intuitive knowledge. However, being overwhelmed with this gift would mean losing track and sight of the gift of spirit and love. Mental intuitive can inspire people and heal the world with innovative inventions and solutions.

Emotional Intuition

Aside from using the mind to make intuitions, you can also be intuitive with the use of emotion.

Emotional Intuitive

They are emotional persons, which experience the world around them through vibrations from things and people. They experience a strong feeling of passion, profound sense of finding the mission in life, connection and a powerful inner experience.

The Influence of an Emotional Intuitive to the Persons Around Him

Emotional intuitives are more inclined on the art of healing. Yet, their energy can be diverted to other choices of career. An emotional intuitive often: triggers the unity among persons; give the people the energy to take action; and ignite the feeling of desire for something.

Side Effects of Being an Emotional Intuitive

An emotional intuitive person tends to absorb energy from others, things, and place. As a result, they will have a roller coaster of emotions. Understanding why a certain emotion is perceived by them is hard. It is simply washing through and over them, which led them to be drained and confused. They are also susceptible to physical sickness such as chronic tiredness, allergies, PMS and adrenal exhaustion. Some also develop uterine and ovary problems.

Staying Healthy and Well Balanced-Emotional Intuitive
Since they use the emotions all time, they are more sensitive to the stimuli of strong scents, crowds and loud noises. This requires them to spend many quiet times and alone moments to refresh themselves. Else, they would be led to the border of panic.

They train themselves to sort out own emotion and those from the outside. They do not define their own emotions by using someone else's emotion. An emotional intuitive can be known as a professional intuitive mentor with friends, yet, it will be risky to mentor a family or a loved one, because it can suck you into their bad moments. Gaining perspective is hard for this portion.

Compatible intuitives

In order to balance an emotional intuitive, a mental intuitive is needed. It is good to have a reasoning behind every emotion. A logic explanation might be need to let an emotional intuitive escape from all the guilt and sadness.

How to make the most out of being an emotional intuitive

Though emotional intuitive makes an incredible motivator and a healer, they also tend to suck the energy of others. Hence, the best thing they can do is to motivate and guide people, which can even move mountains.

Physical Intuition

They understand the world through acts and physical connection with the earth and its creatures.

Physical Intuitive

This kind of intuitives understands the world through tangible or concrete evidences. They are close to the earth and the creatures which constitutes it. They tend to experience: the ability to identify vibrations from physical objects; a strong relationship with the natural world; the processing of the world through the senses; an the knowing of the fact that there is heaven here on earth.

The Influence of a Physical Intuitive to the Persons Around Him

They work to rescue earth creatures and protect the earth, and all its aspects. They aim to transform the world into a place of healing. Their objectives are to rescue animals and forests, and encourage others to do the same thing. They also: awaken the awareness of others regarding our sacred and divine planet; encourage the people to live using their five senses; and provide healing through the use of chiropractic, acupuncture, herbal medicine and traditional medicine.

Side Effects of Being a Physically Intuitive

Due to the fact that they are in-the-moment type of persons, they are more on action and less on speech. They find it hard to put spirituality into words, that is why, they prefer actions. They view spirituality as a concept or a theory and not a thing to include in a schedule or take the time to do it. They absorb physical energy so easily that they tend to experience stomach and lower organ diseases, sudden weight gain, chronic muscular and skeletal ailments and chronic arthritis, fatigue and fibromyalgia.

Staying Healthy and Well Balanced- Physical Intuitive

In order to keep their body healthy, physical intuitives may need to take a full body scan each day. They should locate the areas where there are tense or sores. After locating, they must determine if they are the result of their own stress or the stress of others. Upon knowing the source of stress, it can now be released. Herbal medicine, chiropractic work, homeopathy and massage therapy works well with physical intuitives.

How to Make the Most Out of Being a Physical Intuitive

They tend to believe that they are not into deep intuition, because their way of processing, using actions and touch, seemed to be normal and common to a huge number of people. Yet, their power is not confined to actions and touch, but also the instinctive knowing of the creatures and the earth itself, who needed help. They can be an inspiration to others, if they will embrace the gift given to them.

Spiritual Intuition

The source of their understanding is the opposite of that of the physical intuitives.

Spiritual Intuitive Person

In contrast with those physical intuitives, spiritual intuitives gain understanding through the intangibles. They explore cosmos compared to the actual, physical world. They also: live in a dream world, along with a dream life; rapidly engage themselves in blissful and ecstatic activities; have no destination, goal or agenda; and experiencing visions and precognitive dreams.

The Influence of a Spiritual Intuitive to the Persons Around Him

They make the people around the, aware of the life outside the physical world. They also remind others that a rich spiritual world is out there, waiting to be experienced. They also try to communicate with the spirits on behalf of the physical world. They can also help in toning, chanting and achieving deep trances. They an also perform energy work such as healing touch and Reiki.

Side Effects of Being a Spiritually Intuitive Person

Because of their longing to live in a different world, they find it hard to perform day to day tasks. It seemed difficult for them to connect with the physical world at a tangible degree. This will result to headaches and dizziness, extreme ecstasy which causes indifference and despair, addiction to drugs and alcohol, and glands and thyroid problems.

Staying Healthy and Well Balanced-Spiritual Intuitive

They need to maintain their track in the tangible world. To avoid the feeling of loneliness and being lost, they need to seek the advice of the spiritual leaders and take part of the spiritual community. They also need to make time for healing touch , yoga or massage therapies to balance the energy in their body.

How to make the most out of being a mental intuitive

They tend to have a hard time in understanding the purpose of having a physical world, which makes them hard to approach and connect with other people. Hence, if they known how to maintain in the track of the tangible world, they will be able to balance the connection they make with other people and the spiritual realm.

Mental intuitives make the life mysterious and beautiful because of their belief of another space, which makes us leave the physical world, once in a while.

Chapter 7
How To Think Logically

Have you ever wished to have the ability to solve problems both successfully and easily? If so, be much more rational, you might want to improve your thinking patterns.

Did you see Sherlock's new TV show, played this time by the brilliant Benedict Cumberbatch? If you have, you're probably envy his impressive deduction abilities and thinking, "Why is he doing this?" The truth is you can do it as well.

Okay, maybe you can't solve a complex murder case, but with the objective of promoting problem-solving and decision making, you could improve your logical thinking. In return, these skills will usually lead to your career and life success.

Here are some tricks and techniques that can motivate you to make your mind clearer.

Making Logical Conclusions

Although it may sound stupid to you, try to think in conditional statements and find small and perhaps insignificant facts causes and consequences. For starters, let's say it's cold outside every time it's snowing. The expression would say: "If it snows, outside it's freezing."

If the assumption (the first part of the sentence) is true in conditional sentences, then the inference (the second part) is also true. Attempt to do that with other things also (if I drop my mobile, it's going to get ruined; if I don't eat, I'm going to get starving, etc.) and see if that premise partnership or assumption still fits vice versa.

Play Card Games

Who said it must be difficult to sharpen your logical thinking? It's the reverse. Gather your mates once a week and play card games to stimulate your brain to think easily and clearly. Not only are competitive card games good for the soul and enjoyable, but they can also improve memory, concentration, and analytical skills.

They're much better when you add technique into that mixture. Children can play Crazy Eight or Go Fish fun games, while adults can play Black Jack and Poker.

Make Math Fun

There's no question that math is one of the best exercises to improve your analytical skills. Nevertheless, it can be an unattractive pastime for both children and adults. Fortunately, there are a lot of fun ways to work on your math for you. Through math games on different websites or using smartphone apps, both grown-ups and children can find enjoyment and mental challenges.

Playing Sudoku and other activities that include dealing with numbers in enjoyable and interesting ways will potentially improve the ability of the mind to solve real issues quickly.

Solve Mysteries and Break Codes

Writing crime stories and novels by police allows readers to think critically. Through watching these movies or TV shows, you can get a similar experience. Try to solve a certain mystery before the story's protagonist.

Don't be disappointed if it doesn't go as you expected it would. Just remember from the beginning of this article the words of the famous hero: "When you eliminate the impossible, whatever remains, however unlikely, must be the truth." So remove the impossible and the unlikely, and the solution will come to you. Another great brain activity is cracking codes (created by your buddies or found on the web).

Conduct a Debate

Have you ever been in dispute when you can't find the right arguments to explain why something is good or bad? We've all done it. Debates are good as they allow you to look out causes and consequences, turn them into strong arguments, and find the reasoning behind them all.

Because they need to think logically and make on-the-go decisions, discussions can sharpen your mind. So you can either join a chat group or hold a conversation about economics, art, culture, literature, etc. with your family.

Be Strategic

Since logical thinking is all about putting together the pieces, strategic thinking plays an important role in this process. Being a strategic thinker will not only overcharge the mind, but it will also be a useful asset to work-related choices and even to the success of personal life.

For this reason, some of the fundamental behaviors you can develop are planning (thinking about what is to come), critical thinking (questioning everything), analyzing (seeking patterns), determining (concluding), and improving (from your mistakes). Play strategy games (board games, card games, video games, etc.) and design a strategy for sporting events to sharpen your strategic thinking.

Just as it is important to find your internal peace and focus on your faith, it is also important to keep your mind continually busy with challenging games and activities, so you can develop your rational thinking, which is vital for a productive and therefore harmonious existence.

Evaluate Your Memory

Your brain boosts with workout like any other part of your body. To evaluate your recall is a fantastic method of offering exercise to your brain. See the number of details of a given minute, schedule, or work that you can keep in mind throughout the day.

Try to memorize small things every day. Set up a guide of food and dedicate it to memory as well. Memorize a brief passage from a poem or novel. Wait for an hour and see how much of what you have dedicated to memory you can remember.

Draw a Memory Map.

A map from your home to work, a restaurant, the home of a close friend, or another place you regularly visit.

Notice the Details.

Making a conscious attempt to identify things that are relatively pointless can be a good tool to help you become much more rational. Watch the new journal diminished on the hand of your good friend? Should you list your school and college's actions? Search for mistakes of punctuation in the texts? If the answer is no, it would be a fun time to start at the moment. The more you process, the better your mind is going to be. You're going to end up being a more vital thinker over time.

Other Tricks include:

Based on logical thinking, the reading. Practice in your reading to use inductive or deductive logic — Evite common mistakes.

INDUCTIVE REASONING: You start with several instances (facts or observations) when you reason inductively and use them to draw a general conclusion. You think inductively if you perceive facts. Using the likelihood of generalizing is called an inductive leap. Therefore, inductive claims are intended to produce likely and plausible hypotheses rather than to produce certainty. Your reader draws the inference you hope to draw when your proof mounts. You should ensure that the amount of evidence is adequate and not dependent on analysis that is extraordinary or skewed. Make sure you haven't omitted facts that invalidate the argument (called the "neglected aspect") and given just evidence supporting a predetermined conclusion (called "slanting").

THE TOULMIN Approach: The Toulmin approach is another way to view the mechanism of logical thinking. This model is less restricted than the syllogism and allows for the important elements of probability, support, or proof of the reader's objections ' premise and rebuttal. This approach sees claims as going from agreed facts or evidence (data) to an inference (claim) through an assertion (warrant) forming a fair relationship between the two. The warrant is often implied in arguments, and to be acceptable, as is the unstated premise in the syllogism. The author may cause a big assumption to be expected. Qualifiers like probably, possibly, doubtless, and surely show the degree of certainty of the conclusion; refutational terms like unless the writer allows objections to be anticipated.

FALLACIES: There must be both a plausible and real deductive stated. A real argument is based on well-backed assumptions that are generally accepted. Learn to distinguish between fact and opinion (based on personal preferences) (based on verifiable data). A valid argument fits a pattern of reasonable thought.

Fallacies are flaws in (truth) and logic (validity) assumptions. They may result from misuse or misrepresentation of evidence, relying on defective premises or omitting a necessary premise, or distorting the issues. Some of the major forms of fallacies are as follows:

Non-Sequitur: a statement that does not logically follow from what has just been said; in other words, a conclusion that does not follow from the premises.

Hasty generalization: a generalization based on insufficient evidence or exceptional or biased evidence.

Ad Hominem: Question the individual posing a question rather than dealing with the problem itself objectively.

Bandwagon: An argument that says, "Everyone does and does and believes that, so you should." Red Herring: Dodging the real issue by drawing attention to an irrelevant issue.

Claiming that there are only two options when there are more than two. False Analogy: The belief that in some cases, if two events are the same, they have to be unique. Equivocation: an inference that in two different senses is wrongly dependent on the use of a word.

Slippery Slope: The belief that it will be the first step in a downward spiral if one element is approved.

Oversimplification: A comment or point that leaves relevant issues out.

Pleading for Question: a statement reaffirming the point that has just been made. Such a statement is conditional in that a point mentioned in the assumption is taken as an inference.

Chapter 8
Types of Decision-Making Models

In this chapter, you will learn about the decision-making models or frameworks that you can use to make complex decisions. These are the Rational, Intuitive, and Recognition-Primed decision-making models.

The Rational Decision-Making Model

This is considered to be the classic way of making decisions. It is usually used by decision-makers when they want to make the best decision possible within specific goals and constraints.

When using the rational model, you need to come up with a list of criteria that you will then use to evaluate your options. For example, if you are a top-level manager, this model will provide you with the opportunity to look at the factors that have the greatest impact on your business situation and then select an alternative that reflects company standards.

Every decision-making model has its pros and cons, and the rational model is no different. The biggest benefit of this model is that you are able to set emotions aside and focus on facts. If you value a decision-making process that has structure and discipline, then the rational model is for you. Another benefit is that it is extremely effective when you are given enough time to gather information for deductive reasoning.

On the other hand, the rational model assumes that human beings are rational creatures. Sometimes we are, but oftentimes we are not. The best option that you select may not lead to the right decision, especially when you consider moral/ethical issues as well as the feelings of others. For example, the manager of a company may feel that there is need to move its operations out of one region to boost its revenues. If location is the factor that has the greatest impact on the profitability of the company, then that is the alternative the manager will choose. However, if that decision is made, there will be massive job losses in the region and the local community may lose out in terms of economic development.

Another disadvantage is that the rational model requires a lot of information. We all know that too much information can easily lead to analysis-paralysis. Ultimately, there are times when you are better off going with your gut and ignoring your head.

Intuitive Decision-Making Model

This is also a model often used by managers and experts. Unlike the rational model, the intuitive model appears to be based on instincts and gut feelings. However, upon closer examination, you will realize that this model is actually more sophisticated than that.

Intuition does not necessarily mean relying on feelings alone. If you are an office manager, your intuition will be defined by your years of experience on the job, educational background, skill level, insider information, and many other resources that the average employee will not have access to.

If you are a mother, there are many problems that you solve intuitively. Your intuition will be determined by the number of years you have been raising kids, the amount of time you spend with other mothers, how well you know your kids, and etc. When a situation arises, you don't necessarily panic because somehow you know exactly what to do.

Here is how you apply this model:

- You detect a problem or a situation that needs to be resolved.

- Then you use your intuition to learn the patterns of the problem. There are certain problems that occur in cycles, and this means that there is a specific pattern that is followed. You will have to uncover the *trigger* and the *process* that usually lead to the negative end result.

- Data is then collected to get a better understanding of the problem. This is not an intensive information-gathering process like the rational model. Since you are relying on your intuition, you only collect isolated pieces of data to help you fill in the gaps. You are not collecting information from scratch like someone who doesn't have any idea what to do.

- If there are various solutions or options available, you need to compare and find the one that will produce the best results. Again, picking the best option is done intuitively. Any solution that is counter-intuitive should be eliminated.

- Implement the final solution.

- Examine the situation after solving the problem. Did you pick the best option? Your intuition grows with every experience you go through in life, so this final step will help you improve your decision-making in the future.

As you can see, the intuitive model is more subjective than objective. It relies on your ability to detect patterns and recognize causes and effects of situations. This model is suitable for situations like choosing which restaurant to go to for lunch or which novel to buy.

One of the benefits of the intuitive model is that it leads to faster decision-making. With intuition, you just know what to do, no matter how challenging the situation may seem to others with less experience. Another benefit is that it gives you the opportunity to lean on your personal judgment.

On the other hand, we can also say that the intuitive model depends too much on emotion and personal experience. If your emotions are negative or you have never experienced a particular problem before, you won't know what to do. Your judgment will be clouded, and you will end up making a bad decision based on nothing but impulse. When you assess the situation at the end of it all, you excuse your poor judgment by saying, "I wasn't sure what to do, so I just did what I felt was right."

This is why there is a need for a model that is based on rational facts and figures but also allows the use of your intuition when making everyday decisions.

Recognition Primed Decision-Making Models.

This decision-making model is a combination of rational and intuitive reasoning. This is the model that is often used in life and death situations, especially by people like pilots, military generals and first responders.

If there is one key factor that defines the recognition-primed model and separates it from all the others, it is this: You only assess one option at a time instead of searching for several alternatives.

In the other models, you have to weigh many alternatives at the same time and then select the best one. With this model, you quickly identify the problem and assess its characteristics. These include the goals, cues, expectations, and a potential solution to the problem.

The next step is to think about your plan of action, run a mental scenario, and try to iron out any kinks to the plan. There are two things that can happen at this stage:

- You cannot think of any flaws in your plan of action, so you go ahead and implement it.

- You discover some flaws in your plan and are forced to modify it or pick another solution entirely. You then run the mental simulation again until you get a successful conclusion.

Once you find a solution that can be successfully implemented, according to your mental simulation, you take the necessary action.

The recognition-primed model is very interesting because it is very flexible. For example, if you are an experienced pilot, your ability to recognize patterns will be very high, and this will help you when extrapolating the outcome of your mental scenario. This means that your first solution is likely to be the best decision possible given the situation. The intuition side of the model plays a prominent role.

On the other hand, if you are a young or inexperienced pilot, you haven't faced as many challenges yet, so your ability to recognize problem patterns is low. You have to rely more on the rational side of the model, and you are likely to repeat different scenarios until you get the right solution.

The biggest advantage that this model has is that you can use both intuition and rational reasoning. Your experience also plays a critical role in how you handle a situation. Another benefit is that the mental simulation allows you to 'peer into the future' to learn more about the situation and the flaws that might hinder progress.

On the flip side, this model may not be as suitable for novices or when making non-critical decisions. If you are inexperienced, you may be better off using the rational model. This will help you learn how to gather and process a lot of data at a time. If you are dealing with a non-critical decision, like where to go out on a date, the intuitive model may be best.

Decision-Making Traps

All the above decision-making models can be used effectively depending on your individual situation. But then there is always the possibility of your judgment being clouded despite the model you use. This is the result of what we refer to as decision-making traps.

Here are four of the most common traps that you need to avoid when making decisions:

Confidence Bias – This is a trap that many experienced decision-makers fall into. Most companies value managers who are confident in their abilities and cool under pressure. However, if the manager becomes overconfident due to past successes, they can become careless and make risky decisions. Confidence bias can make you oversimplify a situation or even miss certain key details, and in our case, the manager's decision will cost the company.

The solution to confidence bias is to pause, step back from the situation, and look at it through an objective lens. Do not be too quick to rely on your personal opinions or past experiences.

Hindsight Bias – This is where you rely on past events to judge current problems. For example, when a problem occurs, the right thing to do is to identify the person, event, or item that led to that particular situation. If you are walking down the hall and trip over a skateboard, you will want to know which one of your three kids left it there in the first place. You know that your eldest son owns the skateboard and is the one who is always forgetting to put it away. It's not the first time this has happened, so naturally, you blame him and decide to punish him.

This is hindsight bias because you are being selective in your view of the situation. Instead of finding out the events that led to the skateboard being left in the hallway, you rely on past events and end up making the wrong decision. With a little digging, you would have discovered that it's your youngest daughter who stole the skateboard from her brother's room, played with it, and forgot to return it!

The biggest danger with hindsight bias is that it can quickly escalate into internal conflict, accusations, and counter-accusations.

> **Anchoring Bias** – This occurs when you make decisions based on specific information that you want to see instead of all the evidence available. You might end up ignoring other alternatives that would have led to a better solution.

For example, a CEO of a company asks his manager to find out why sales are dropping. The CEO has always had a feeling that his sales team is lazy and doesn't give their all to push company products. After some research, the manager presents a range of possible causes to the CEO, including poor customer service, lack of effective marketing and advertising, poor product design, and laxity in the sales department.

It doesn't take long for the CEO to determine where the problem is. It must be the sales team. Why? Because he is only focusing on the information that he wants to see. All the other potential causes don't even deserve a second look. He has found information to anchor his decision on. This kind of trap can distort the problem and lead to wrong solutions.

> 4. Escalation of Commitment – Once you make a decision, you want to stick with it, right? So, if somebody came and told you that your decision is flawed, it is likely that you would become defensive. Nobody likes to be told that they are wrong.

If you are a manager in a company, you would probably claim that your plan is failing because employees are not committing enough time and energy into executing your decision. Instead of looking at the facts and admitting you made the wrong decision, you end up committing more resources to a terrible plan.

This is the fatal trap known as escalation of commitment. You increase your commitment to a bad decision simply because you feel too embarrassed to change course.

If you want to make better decisions, you need to learn how to use the right model in every situation. Then you must commit to frequent practice to avoid the traps above.

Chapter 9
7 Key Strategies to Improve Problem Solving and Logical Thinking

Critical thinking is all about solving problems, using logical thinking as a guide. When your logical thinking happens to be flawed, then you will find that solving problems can be a challenge, and that the decisions you make will not be good. Now that you know how to develop your critical thinking skills, you need some guidance on improving these skills so that they can be perfected over time. The end result is that instead of spending too much time thinking hard about a problem, you will be able to think better. Here are 7 key strategies that will guarantee you positive results with problem solving as well as logical thinking.

Delve Deeper into the Question

Starting off with a broad question will make it difficult for you to come up with the right answer, particularly when you are thinking critically.

Critical thinking calls for you to examine a host of variables, following which you are then able to get to a solution. Here is an example of how you can delve deeper.

Question 1 – How can I teach a class?

This question is challenging to respond to as there are many variables that have not been explained. These include the size of the class, the type of class, the educational level and so on. Attempting to logically address this will lead you to confusion.

Question 2 – How can I teach a high school English class with 10 students?

This question is much better than the first question. It brings in certain specifics including the education level, the subject of the class and the number of students. From this, you can begin to logically come up with a solution. However, you can do even better when delving deeper into the question.

Question 3 – What are the number of high school students taking English this semester? How can I teach a high school English class with 10 students?

This helps put your response in better perspective such that you can now break your logical response into several problems. From these problems, you are better able to determine what they are attributed to such that they begin to make better sense as you continue with your critical analysis of the issue at hand.

Make Use of Diagrams

A picture speaks a thousand words and an excellent diagram can help to accentuate your logical thinking. A great mind that embodied an excellent critical thinker was Steve Jobs from Apple. When sharing information in a presentation, he drew the audience in and helped them arrive at a conclusion by making use of illustrations and diagrams in his presentations. The type of diagrams that you should lean towards include flow charts that lay out processes, boxes which can contain information as well as represent your logic. When you have a problem to solve, try drawing it out first using a paper and pan, and then, you can apply the necessary words to find a solution. Over time, you will be able to mentally create your own flowcharts and diagrams, and influence your decision making without the need for other materials.

Attempt Logical Games

There are games that are purely based on logic if you want to arrive at a solution, such as chess and Sudoku. Chess is a great game to play with another person, as you learn to understand how other people think, and how their thoughts affect their judgements. You also develop the skills of strategy and problem solving, as you work your way across the board in an attempt to win the game.

Sudoku is a great game to play on your own, as it helps you come up with different ways that you can reason. Through this game, you learn about solving a problem by getting rid of certain variables, and using the information that you have available to help you arrive at a viable solution.

Consider your Assumptions

You will be amazed at the number of assumptions that you make before you finally arrive at a decision. Assumptions are not based on truth or something that must happen, they are instead our opinions of something that could happen if we take a certain action. When looking to improve your problem solving and logical thinking abilities, you need to be discern when your thoughts and actions are based on assumptions instead of facts. This means that you need to be able to dissect the issue.

Consider the following assumption – You go to sleep at night because you are tired. Here the assumption is that in order for you to go to sleep, you must be tired. This may not be the case. Rather than basing a result on a conclusion of this nature, it would be better to examine it more deeply, to determine the real reasons that lead to sleep, and whether this is linked to the reasons that cause one to be tired.

Choose the Right People Around You

Many people who are successful do not make it to the top because they are brilliant, they make it to the top because they are willing to invest in and hire people who are more intelligent than they are. This means that they have the best minds operating their businesses, while at the same time, they remain motivated to get the knowledge required to keep up with their staff.

When you have people smarter than you around you, it is easier to learn something from them, which will help you improve the way that you do

things, as well as build on your critical thinking skills. Their intelligence will make it necessary for you to come up with logical ways to interact and communicate with them, which will help develop the way that your brain works as well.

Read Logical Books

Read, read and read some more, and you will be amazed at how quickly you can elevate your logical reasoning. Do not read just any books. Focus on those that will get you thinking, and these books mainly fall into the category of mysteries and thrillers. As you read these books, work on figuring out what could happen by the end of the book. You may need to identify a villain, figure out what is happening with an attack, or simple solve a mystery of some sort. By looking at all the variables, you will find that making a calculated guess is not only possible, it gets easier with time. To perfect this skill, you must keep reading and keep practicing.

Investigate Everything

Every time that you receive some information, take time to do a thorough investigation to determine whether the information that you have on hand is good or not. This is applicable to all information, no matter who the source may be. When you being to investigate in this matter, your brain starts to analyze information in a different way. You will begin to see loopholes in information, and make judgements based on all that has been made available to you. This is particularly true of negative news which may be sensational rather than factual. Problem solving will become much easier, as will critical thinking when it comes to addressing issues.

These seven strategies are highly practical and easy to implement. They are also result oriented, and the more you practice them, the easier it becomes to be a critical thinker.

Chapter 10
The Power of Critical Observation

Our ability to systematically observe and rigorously screen our environment for clues and information to help us make better decisions is decreasing at an alarming rate. This is unfortunate as this skill, which I call critical observation, is a powerful tool for becoming more successful. Critical observation provides us with the clues, insights, and relevant information that make our decisions and strategies more successful. It can help us detect risks and opportunities before others do. In fact, most risk catastrophes (such as financial crises, wars, political and social disruptions) are preceded by warning signs and red flags clearly visible to those practicing critical observation.

Critical observation is therefore one of the most important items in the critical thinking toolbox. It is a technique to be mastered before moving on to the black belt classes of critical thinking. Critical observation forces us to look at reality systematically with great focus before making important decisions. This reality check helps us to unmask myths, false ideas and beliefs, wrong assessments, and unjustified claims that could contribute to poor decision making.

Being a critical observer of reality differentiates us from those who base their decisions on superficial, incomplete, or incorrect observations. An experienced critical observer can gain three distinctive advantages:

- Reality becomes less complex and less opaque,
- Life outcomes and the forces that determine them become more understandable and more predictable,
- Being caught unprepared by adverse surprises becomes less likely.

Critical observation focuses on four groups of insights:

1. Meaningful patterns and anomalies,
2. Relevant correlations, interdependencies, and potential causalities,
3. New or previously undetected trends and changes in our environment and, more generally,
4. New information on relevant issues.

Critical observation has played a decisive role in many medical breakthroughs, technological innovations, and business and investment successes. It not only increases the effectiveness of critical thinking, it also advances analysis to decision making.

Unfortunately, the tool of critical observation is not used commonly. Most of us are in a state of reduced awareness and partial blindness. Constant distraction by phones, internet, social media, television, and other diversions, as well as our passivity and cognitive laziness, results in our missing relevant information that could help us understand reality and make better decisions. We are trapped in a world of superficial observation and distraction leading to a false, biased, and incomplete understanding of reality.

> Quick exercise to test our awareness and alertness:
>
> Test 1:
>
> Think back to the last three business meetings you attended. Describe the mood of each person when the meeting ended; if it was a large group, name three people who seemed unhappy at the end of the meeting.
>
> Test 2:
>
> Can you remember the full names and professional backgrounds of the last twenty people whom you met?

Most people cannot complete these exercises. They are too distracted to pay attention to people or to remember their names and professional backgrounds. This is in sharp contrast to highly successful people. They are alert, screening their environment for new information that could give them a competitive edge. For example, one successful top manager carries always a little

Dictaphone in his pocket to record immediately any relevant observation. He carefully archived observations for later reference. His radar is always on. He does not miss an important observation.

Most people miss out on the advantages of critical observation. They ignore the many sources of information around them that could improve their decision making. Superficial observation leads to serious negative consequences:

- We fail to detect valuable clues, information, and insights that could improve our understanding of reality and could result in better decision making.

- We fail to anticipate risks and opportunities.

- Our unawareness and misunderstanding of reality expose us to dangerous levels of unpreparedness and vulnerability.

- We can easily be manipulated by others.

Real world example:

I often witness young professionals in giving business presentations. The most common mistake they make is not observing the audience. This lack of critical observation often endangers the success of their work. They fail to detect highly important information: Do the listeners understand the points I make? Do they agree? Do the top decision makers in

> *the audience agree? Should I slow down and repeat a crucial argument? Is the audience bored; should I move faster? The best content does not help if the audience disagrees with the main points or simply does not understand the key messages. Critical observation of the audience helps to keep a high level of engagement.*

To avoid the negative consequences of superficial observation of our environments, we must develop and train our critical observation skills. Here is a practice example that addresses a common problem: how to lose weight and live a healthier life. For me, critical thinking played a decisive role in tackling this problem.

In 2010, a routine checkup encouraged me to tackle two issues: losing weight and rectifying some negative health parameters. While my overall state of health was good, I decided that actions had to be taken to avoid more serious problems in the future.

If you want to lose weight and improve your health, you easily find yourself in a confusing and frustrating situation. When you type "healthy living" into the search box of Amazon books, you receive more than 60,000 responses. There are many medications and supplements to help you achieve certain goals. But the frustration and confusion does not stop here. The recommendations given by health experts are often contradictory and change over time. Therefore, it is not surprising that many people fail to achieve their health and weight loss goals simply because they are confused by a cacophony of contradictory information and recommendations.

I decided to create my own health program based on critical observation of reality. There are many people around me who are busy but managed to stay lean and healthy. My hypothesis was that I have to study these positive role models and learn (with some adjustments) from their strategies and habits. Obviously, I would use critical thinking to double-check the validity of my observations and conclusions.

I focused on three core activities:

- Use critical observation to identify positive and negative role models and study their habits and behavior in great detail (i.e., eating preferences and habits, exercise behavior, speed, frequency, and timing of eating). In other words, I started doing my own research based on my own observations of reality.

- Based on these critical observations, I built hypotheses to explain the difference between positive and negative role models. More specifically, I tried to find concrete differences between healthy and unhealthy people that explain the different outcomes.

- Observe the situational context that may impact the behavior and outcomes of studied individuals.

Critical observation needs to be diligent and thorough. The more focused the observation, the more valuable the results. My observations of positive and negative role models were gathered using a wide spectrum of observation activities.

Employing *Critical Observation* to identify healthier lifestyle choices – Illustrative case example

Selection of activities
<ul><li>Analyze case studies of the elderly. What differentiates positive and negative role models? A special focus was given to those older people who were particularly vital, energetic, healthy, and mentally sharp. I found them among family members, colleagues, friends, and biographies of famous people.</li><li>Scrutinize the shopping carts in grocery stores of people who appear to be positive or negative role models. What are the key differences?</li><li>Observe the behavior of colleagues at work (snacking behavior, what/how much they ate at business dinners, do they have dessert? How fast do they eat?).</li></ul>

> - Find turnabout examples (people who significantly improved their overall health: what were the key changes in their lives).
> - What do successful, healthy top managers eat? What are their lifestyle choices?

I was astonished by how quickly I identified significant behavioral differences between the positive and negative role models. Success or failure did not seem to be accidental. A critical observer could easily find different lifestyle and nutrition choices between the two groups. I also noticed that positive role models were not only healthier. They were more energetic, less moody, happier, and more successful. This observation created additional motivation for me to change my nutrition and lifestyle choices dramatically.

I summarized my observations and conclusions in a personalized health program that was tailored to my goals, needs, and restrictions. The results were impressive. Not only did I achieve all of my health goals, I surpassed many of my goals by a wide margin.

Critical observation can be applied in all aspects of life. We know famous fictional detectives, such as Sherlock Holmes and Colombo, who used critical observation to find the decisive clues to solve complex criminal cases. Often, these decisive clues were not seen by the superficial observer. Critical observation was required to detect them.

Many famous scientists, military leaders, business people, and investors owe their success to their ability to conduct critical observation. Many breakthroughs in science, technology, and business were achieved through critical observation.

Breakthroughs enabled by *Critical Observation*

Major science/innovation breakthroughs made possible by *Critical Observation*
- Alexander Fleming: Observed that accidental mold build-up in an experiment killed bacteria and went on to develop penicillin. - Isaac Newton: Understood gravity by observing an apple falling from a tree. - Konrad Lorenz: Detected behavioral and social patterns by critically observing nature and in particular graylag geese. He was awarded the Nobel Prize in 1973. - Darwin: Developed theory of evolution based on critical observations of nature. - George de Mestral: Observed seeds stuck to his clothes on a hunting trip, using a reversible hook

> and loop system. This observation led to the development of the Velcro fastening system.

The discovery of penicillin by Scottish scientist Alexander Fleming is interesting, as it shows that critical observation can lead to accidental discoveries. Returning to his laboratory from vacation, Fleming realized that fungus grew in one of his experimental cultures. He probably had failed to close the container properly before he left the laboratory. Many would have thrown the contaminated container in the trash, but Fleming took a closer look and made an historic observation. He realized that the staphylococci bacteria close to the fungus died, while the bacteria farther away from the mold survived. This observation led to the development of penicillin, a powerful antibiotic that has saved millions of lives.

Austrian Nobel Prize winner Konrad Lorenz used critical observation as a core research tool. Lorenz studied behavioral aspects of humans and animals. He became famous for his work observing the behavior of graylag geese and detecting several forms of instinctive behavior. For example, his observations showed that young graylag geese bond with the first moving object they sense after hatching whether this object was the mother goose or a human.

Lorenz' discoveries could not have been made by any other research method at that time. Only focused critical observation allowed him to decode human and animal behavior.

George de Mestral is another great example of the power of critical observation. Others brushed seeds off their clothes after walking through bushes in a forest; de Mestral, however, did not. He was curious why some seeds could stick so effectively to his clothes and dog but were easy to remove by hand. Using a microscope, he discovered a powerful natural hook and loop system. This observation led to the invention of the Velcro fastening system, which made de Mestral famous.

Critical observation, whether conducted purposefully (Lorenz) or not (Fleming), is often the decisive steppingstone to success. We should recognize this and limit the distractions that blur our understanding of the world. The following suggestions may help you build your critical observation skills.

HOW TO GET STARTED WITH CRITICAL OBSERVATION

For many of us caught in a world of superficial observation, it may be difficult to switch to a more active, alert, and focused way of observation. Time and patience are required.

The following chart lists some of the requirements for successful critical observation.

Requirements for successful *Critical Observation*

Critical Observation: getting started	
• Curiosity • Patience/time • Open-mindedness • Willingness to ask questions/formulate hypotheses • Observe objects and situations from varying perspectives • Constant cycle of observing, hypotheses building, testing, and refining hypotheses	• Courage to challenge status quo • Constructive skepticism • Training in pattern recognition • Constant radar screening of our environment for material clues • Alternate between macroscopic and microscopic observation

A change in perspective is important to the practice of critical observation. This includes looking at an issue from different angles, alternating between a microscopic view (detailed focusing on a small area) and a macroscopic view (looking at the bigger picture). Switching from a microscopic to a macroscopic perspective may lead to deeper insights into how things work.

The following chart provides a framework for organizing and directing critical observation projects.

Organizing our *Critical Observation* activities

Activity	**Goal**
Screen	• 360-degree screening of environment to gather relevant information
Detect	• Patterns, trends, causalities, interdependencies, correlations
Compare	• Compare sample observations with those from the past, different locations and societies
Challenge and Question	• Challenge status quo and conventional wisdom • Explore alternative explanations

Conclude	• Build new hypotheses based on insights gained

Critical observation has helped me gain important insights into how things work. For example, it helped me succeed professionally in different countries, cultures, industries, and circumstances. The insights generated by critical observations were the foundation of many important decisions in my personal and professional lives.

Taking a case study as a management consultant, critical observation enabled me to:

- Identify dangerous risks and attractive opportunities
- Identify opportunities for operational improvements for my clients
- Identify and anticipate new trends, disruptions, and developments more quickly
- Gain new insights that resulted in a change in strategy, tactics, or behavior

As a result, I was able to build a track record that helped me gain the trust of my clients. It also improved anticipation of challenges and threats to prepare my clients appropriately. In this context, I developed a new approach for my clients: *future anticipation*. It uses critical observation and critical thinking to identify forces and trends that will shape future outcomes. Systematically identifying a wide range of possible future scenarios (and preparing proactively for their impact on us) greatly reduces the chances of being caught unprepared. In fact, doing so often creates a valuable and sustainable competitive advantage over a company's competition.

The following example illustrates the concept of future anticipation using both critical observation and critical thinking.

> ***Real world case example: how critical observation helped me anticipate the financial crisis of 2007***
>
> In late 1999, I observed activities in the U.S. credit markets that made me curious. I was working as a management consultant in New York and developed a particular interest in risk management topics. The following critical observations raised some questions for me:
>
> - While U.S. indebtedness reached record levels, it was getting easier to get credit (loans and mortgages). Some banks advertised that they would approve your loan "while you wait."
>
> - Banks entertained the idea of drastically downsizing credit risk management staff as they felt less need to analyze credit risk.

- Banks' incentive systems strongly encouraged employees to originate new mortgages and loans (with less effort on analyzing credit risk). This happened in the context of new bank strategies that focused on repackaging and trading credit risk rather than keeping it (a technique also known as securitization).

- My mailbox was flooded with preapproved mortgage and credit card advertisements. This was just a few years after having experienced problems getting approved for a credit card (due to not having credit history in the U.S.).

- Friends moving to Manhattan told me that they bought an apartment (facilitated by a large mortgage) instead of renting one, as renting was too expensive.

These observations did not make sense. I knew from my experience in risk management that credit risk is a so-called long tail risk. Loans made in good times can easily default during bad times (many years after the origination of the loan). Therefore, to treat credit risk as a short-term risk creates a future problem.

I initiated a research project to analyze the long-term stability of the U.S. banking and credit markets. This project confirmed

> my initial hypotheses as it identified serious deficiencies in the way credit risk was measured and managed in the U.S.
>
> These deficiencies created substantial and sometimes hidden credit risks that could lead to massive losses in the long term. In fact, the results of my research project suggested that a severe financial crisis was likely if these deficiencies remained unaddressed, leading to poorly managed credit risks. In other words, it was only a question of time until the banking system would experience a severe crisis.
>
> Unfortunately, instead of addressing the issues identified, financial institutions accelerated their efforts to originate and repackage credit risk in the years following my research. While benign market conditions helped for a few years, the U.S. financial system was eventually hit by a severe crisis in 2007. Due to my dedication to critical observation, I was able to raise this issue with many clients long before the crisis.

Critical observation helped me anticipate the financial crisis of 2007 and warn clients to prepare for it. It was a good example of the use of critical observation to anticipate potential risks.

Therefore, I highly encourage learning and practicing this skill. You can do it alone, with a friend, or with a group. A group may provide additional benefits as people make different observations.

Chapter 11
Psychology of Arguments

What is argumentation and why is it important?

The term "argumentation" comes from the Latin word "argumentatio", which means "casting arguments". This means that we bring any prove in order to arouse trust or sympathy for the thesis, hypothesis or statement put forward by us. The complex of such proves is the argument.

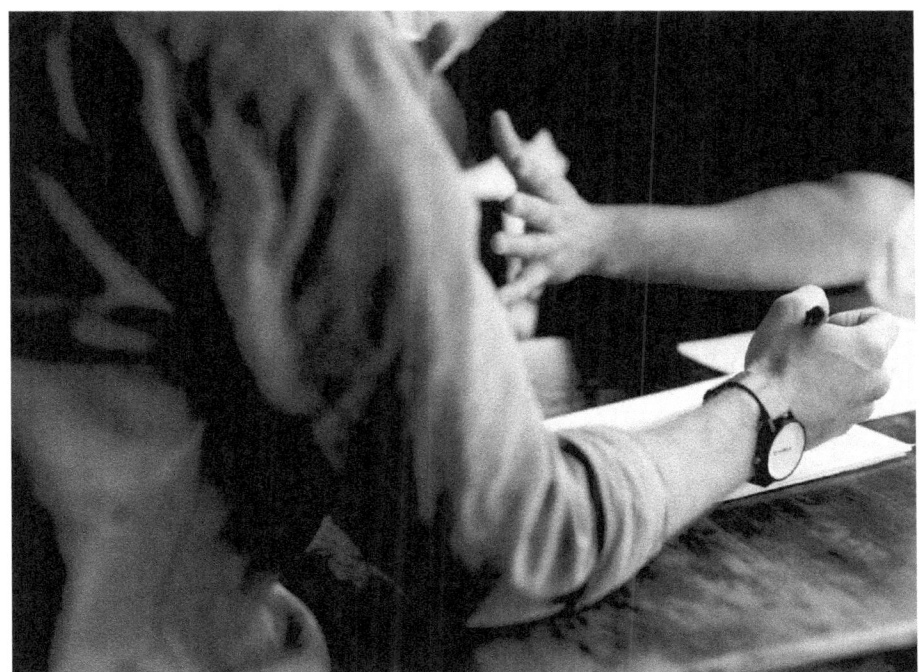

The purpose of argumentation is to make the addressee accept the theory put forward by the author. And by and large, the argument can be called an interdisciplinary study of conclusions as the result of logical reasoning. The argument takes place in the scientific, and in the domestic, and in the legal, and in the political sphere; always used in conversations, dialogs, beliefs, negotiations, etc.

The ultimate goal of argumentation is to convince the audience of the truth of a situation, induce people to accept the author's point of view, and encourage them to think or act.

Argumentation is a historical phenomenon, and it changes over time. For its expression are linguistic means, for example, pronounced or written statements. These statements, their interrelationships and their influence on a person are studied by the theory of argumentation.

Argumentation is purposeful activity, and it can both strengthen and weaken one's beliefs. This is also a social activity, because when a person argues his position, he acts on those with whom he contacts. This implies dialogue and the active reaction of the opposite side to evidence. In addition, it is assumed that the interlocutor is adequate, and his ability to rationally weigh the arguments, accept them or challenge them.

It is thanks to argumentation that a person can intelligibly explain to someone his point of view, confirm its truthfulness with good reason, and eliminate misunderstanding. Well-reasoned judgments minimize doubt, talk about the veracity and seriousness of the hypotheses, assumptions and statements made. Moreover, if a person is able to make good arguments in his favor, this serves as an indicator that he has repeatedly criticized all the information he has.

For the same reason, trust should only be given to information that can be reasonably argued. This will mean that they are verified, proven and true (or at least an attempt to do so has been made). Actually, this is the goal of critical thinking - to question something in order to find supporting or disproving facts.

From all of the above, we can conclude that argumentation is the most correct and open way to influence the opinions and decisions of other people. Naturally, for teaching critical thinking to give results, and for argumentation to be effective, it is necessary to know not only theoretical, but also its practical foundations.

Our lives revolve around language. We use it to assert facts, pose queries, instruct others, commend or affront, swear to accomplish something, convey a story, make threats, and even sing songs. We use language to persuade or influence other people. But, people do not always attempt to influence others through argument. Some people attempt to persuade others by using rhetorical means.

The critical thing that you need to realize is that when you use arguments to try and persuade others, you present valid justifications for accepting a particular claim. An argument appeals to critical faculties and logical reasoning. Rhetorical methods, in contrast, tend to depend on the convincing power of specific words and verbal strategies to induce others to accept your convictions, desires, and actions. Instead of appealing to a person's critical faculties, rhetorical methods appeal to yearnings, worries, and other human emotions.

You should be aware that there are valid arguments that are not necessarily worthy arguments. It may be detrimental to you or to another person if you rashly dismiss those bad but valid arguments, so it is important that you also learn how to analyze attempts to influence to see if they are indeed valid or not. You can perform this analysis in three main steps.

The first step is a critical one because it entails discerning whether the idea being presented to you is indeed an argument. You need to ascertain the exact issue that is being discussed, and you need to discern whether the person you are discussing it with is trying to influence you through argument or not.

After you have determined that the idea being presented to you is an argument, you can then progress to the next step of restructuring the argument so you can understand it in a clearer manner. This will aid you in breaking down the various elements or components of the argument to see if there are any errors or inaccuracies.

After you have restructured the argument, the first and last step is to evaluate it by asking questions such as, "What is good or bad about this argument?" You need to look at the argument from an objective point of view without letting your personal belief system hinder you from coming up with clear and logical justifications.

The Structure of Arguments and Communications

Critical thinkers must learn about how people use speech and ideas in order to be able to effectively and accurately evaluate them for validity and for soundness. The English language offers lots of opportunities for faulty argumentation and poor speech patterns and the critical thinker must work diligently in order to evaluate and assess when there is a potential problem with a piece of communication. Let's begin by looking at two types of reasoning.

Deductive Reasoning

Deductive arguments move from general statements to a specific statement. They are valid if the general statements are true. Consider this example:

> **All birds lay eggs, and ostriches are birds. Therefore, ostriches lay eggs.**

Conclusions based upon deductive reasoning are always going to be true if the premises are true. If the premises are untrue, the argument may still be valid even though the conclusion may be untrue. Consider the following example:

> **All humans over seventy-five years of age suffer from dementia. Rudy is seventy-nine years old. Therefore, Rudy suffers from dementia.**

Logically speaking, the above example is a valid statement that uses deductive reasoning. However, even though the argument is valid, its conclusion is untrue because not everyone over the age of seventy-five suffers from dementia.

Inductive Reasoning

Inductive reasoning is the opposite of deductive reasoning because instead of moving from the general to specific, inductive reasoning looks at specific situations and attempts to make generalizations about them. Consider the following examples:

> **David is a pastor, and he is an honest man. Therefore, all pastors are honest men.**

or:

This is a container of gasoline. When I drop this match into the container, the gasoline catches on fire. Therefore, gasoline is flammable.

Scientists use inductive reasoning to build theories all of the time regarding how two or more variables work together. However, it is important to note that even though the first two statements, or premises, in an inductive reasoning statement may be true, it does not necessarily mean that the conclusion will be true.

One of your missions as a critical thinker is to evaluate the premises being presented as factual in a given argument and then make a judgment about the truthfulness and the validity of those premises. Often, the arguments you will hear or read will be much more complex than the ones illustrated here. For that reason, it is helpful to break down arguments into smaller and more manageable structures so that you can evaluate them easier.

Troublesome Words and Phrases

As a critical thinker, one of your goals should be to communicate in ways in which the message you are delivering is clear and precise. All too often, people are ambiguous or vague in their speech, which can lead to some confusion as one attempts to interpret what the communicator is actually saying or asking.

Vagueness

Words or phrases that are vague are imprecise or unclear. Consider the following scenario: you have just finished taking a final World History course and Jan, your best friend, is considering taking the course for the upcoming semester. Jan calls you on the phone and says:

"Hi. I heard that you took the World History course. Is it difficult?"

Can you spot the problem in Jan's question to you? The issue lies with the word, "difficult," because even though you might have found the course to be relatively easy because you have studied world history in the past, Jan may find the course more "difficult" because she has not taken a world history course before at the college level. Not everyone who takes the World History course will perceive it as having the same degree of difficulty and so in order to answer Jan's question with any degree of accuracy, you have to probe a bit to learn what sort of criteria would make the course difficult for your friend and then reflect about the course and share that information with her.

As a student and as a practitioner of critical thought, you are charged with the task of minimizing your use of vague terms or phrases in your speech and in your writing. In addition, practicing critical thinkers strive to identify vagueness when they encounter it in the communications of others and then seek to clarify exactly what is being communicated through questioning the person providing the information. Vagueness in communication allows for misinterpretation, which is something critical thinkers strive to avoid as much as possible.

So, in our scenario above, if you were sincerely interested in answering Jan's question with any degree of accuracy, you would have to ask her to be more specific about what she was asking. In other words, you would have to get her to tell you what specific criteria would render the World History course difficult for her, and then let her know whether that criteria exists in the curriculum of the course or not.

Ambiguity

Ambiguous words or phrases can have more than one meaning and are thus unclear. Ambiguity is similar to vagueness because they both create communication obstacles that cause a lack of clarity or precision to be present. Here is a simple example:

Billy, your trusted coworker, comes by your desk on a Tuesday morning and says:

"Joanne, the new account manager, is very green."

You look up at Billy and you wonder if Joanne's skin has a green pallor to it, or if Billy is referring to Joanne's inexperience with the work she is assigned to do. Here's another example:

Billy, the same coworker, is describing a boxing match he watched on television over the weekend and says:

"Simpson hit Jackson hard and then he began bleeding bad."

Again, you look at Billy curiously and have to ask yourself who, specifically, was bleeding: Simpson, or Jackson?

Your role as a critically thinking communicator is to work to make sure that the words, phrases, and sentences you choose to use are unambiguous. If the words or phrases you choose can be interpreted more than one way, you need to clarify how you wish the reader or listener to interpret it with a short explanation. If at all possible, your goal should be to remove all ambiguity from your sentences and phrases.

The practical basis of argumentation

The scope of the concept of "argumentation" is very deep. Given that this is perhaps the most difficult of the stages of persuasion, it requires a person to have knowledge and possession of material, endurance and ability to concentrate, assertiveness and correctness of statements. It should be remembered that the author of the arguments always depends on his interlocutor, because the latter will decide whether arguments are acceptable to him or not.

Argumentation has its own structure. It looks like this:

• Thesis - the wording of your position, proposal or opinion.

• Making arguments - this includes evidence, evidence and arguments by which the author substantiates his position (the arguments should explain why the interlocutor should trust you or agree with you).

• Demonstration - this refers to a demonstration of the relationship of the thesis with arguments (it is at this stage that the conviction is achieved).

With the help of argumentation, you can partially or completely change the opinion and point of view of the interlocutor. However, to succeed, you need to follow a few important rules:

• You need to operate with convincing, accurate, clear and simple concepts.

• The information must be true (if the reliability of the data is not established, then you do not need to use them until everything is checked).

• During the conversation, you need to choose a specific pace and specific methods of argumentation, based on the characteristics of your character and temperament.

• All arguments must be correct; no personal attacks are allowed.

- It is recommended to refrain from using non-business statements that make it difficult to understand information; it is better to operate with visual arguments; when covering negative information, its source must be indicated.

For a person who is well acquainted with what he is talking about, it will not be difficult to find good arguments. But most often, if there is a task to convince your interlocutor, it is better to stock up with convincing arguments in advance. For example, you can sketch out a list of them, and then analyze and determine the most effective ones. But here you should know how to identify strong and weak arguments. This is done using the criteria for their assessment:

- Effective arguments are always factual. Based on this, from a list compiled in advance, you can immediately discard information that cannot be supported by facts.

- Effective arguments are always directly related to the subject of discussion. All other arguments should be excluded.

- Effective arguments are always relevant to the interlocutor. For this reason, you need to find out in advance what interest the arguments will be for the addressee.

If you are sure that your arguments meet the proposed criteria, you can proceed directly to the argument. Based on this, the development of critical thinking involves mastering of basic methods of argumentation.

Chapter 12
Basic Argumentation Methods

Argumentation theory suggests using quite a lot of argumentation methods. We will talk about the most effective of them. They are suitable for both business and everyday communication.

Fundamental method

The meaning of the method is a direct appeal to the person whom you want to acquaint with facts that represent the basis of your conclusions.

Of greatest importance here is the digital and statistical information, which serves as an ideal background for confirming the arguments. Unlike verbal (and often controversial) data, numbers and statistics are much more convincing and objective.

But the use of such information does not need to be too zealous. Too many digits act tiringly, as a result of which the arguments lose their effect. It is also important that incorrect data can lead the listener astray.

Ignore method

Most often, ignoring is used in disputes and conversations. The meaning is this: if you cannot refute the fact offered by your opponent, you can successfully ignore its meaning and value. When you see that a person attaches importance to something that, in your opinion, is not of particular importance, you simply ignore it.

Contradiction method

For the most part, this method can be called protective. Its basis is to identify contradictions in the arguments of the opponent and focus on them. As a result, if his arguments are unfounded, you will easily win.

Method "Yes, but"

The presented method gives the best results when the opponent prejudices the topic of conversation. Given that objects, phenomena and processes have both positive and negative sides, this method makes it possible to see and discuss alternative ways to solve the problem.

Comparison method

This method is highly efficient because makes the author's speech bright and impressive. Also, this method can be called one of the forms of the method of "extraction of conclusions." Thanks to him, the argument becomes weighty and explicit. For amplification, it is recommended to use well-known analogies with phenomena and objects.

Method "Boomerang"

The "Boomerang" method allows you to use the opponent's own "weapon" against him. The method lacks evidentiary power, but despite this, it most seriously affects the listener, especially if wit is used.

Partial argumentation method

This is one of the most popular methods. The meaning of this method is that the opponent's monologue is divided into clearly distinguishable parts using the phrases "this is clearly wrong", "you can look at this question differently," "that's for sure," etc.

Interestingly, the basis of the method is the well-known thesis: if in any argument and conclusion you can always find something dubious or unreliable, then confident pressure on the interlocutor allows us to clarify even the most difficult situation.

Method of visible support

Refers to the methods for the application of which you need to prepare. This method can be used in situations when you are an opponent, for example, in a dispute. The essence of the method is as follows: for example, the interlocutor voiced his arguments to you about the problem being discussed, and the word passes to you. Here lies the trick: at the beginning of your argument you do not say anything in opposition to the words of your opponent; you even bring new arguments in support of him, surprising everyone in this.

But this is just an illusion, because a counterattack will follow. It is carried out approximately according to the following scheme: "But .... in support of your point of view, you forgot to give a few other facts ... (list these facts), and that's not all, because ... "(Your arguments and proofs follow).

Your ability to think critically and to argue your position will seriously develop, even if you limit yourself to mastering the above methods. However, if your goal is to achieve professionalism in this field, this will be extremely small. To begin to move on, you need to study the other components of argumentation. The first of these is the rules of argumentation.

Argumentation rules

The rules of argumentation are quite simple, but each of them differs in a set of its features. There are four of these rules:

Rule one

Operate with convincing, precise, clear and simple terms. Keep in mind that persuasiveness is easily lost if the arguments presented are vague and abstract. Also take into account that in most cases people catch and understand much less than they want to show.

Rule two

It is advisable to choose the method of argumentation and its pace in accordance with the characteristics of your temperament. This rule assumes:

• Testimonies and facts, presented separately, are more effective than those presented collectively.

• Several (three to five) of the most vivid arguments are more effective than many average facts.

• Argumentation should not be in the form of a "heroic" monologue or declaration.

• Using well-placed pauses, you can achieve a better result than using a stream of words.

• An active rather than a passive construction of statements has a greater impact on the interlocutor, especially when it is necessary to provide evidence (for example, the phrase "we will do this" is much better than the phrase "we can do this", etc.).

Rule three

The argument should always look correct. It means:

• If the person is right, admit it openly, even if the consequences may be unfavorable to you.

• If the interlocutor has accepted any arguments, try to use them in the future.

• Avoid dummy phrases that indicate a decrease in concentration and lead to inappropriate pauses to gain time or search for a thread of conversation (such phrases may be: "it was not said", "it can be and so and so", "in other words", "more or less," "as I said," etc.).

Rule four

Adapt the arguments to the person of the interlocutor:

• Build argumentation, taking into account the motives and goals of the opponent.

• Remember that the so-called "excessive" persuasiveness can cause opposition from the opponent

• Avoid using words that makes it difficult to understand and reason.

- Strive for the most visual presentation of your evidence, considerations and ideas with examples and comparisons, but remember that they should not be at variance with the interlocutor's experience, that is, should be close and understandable to him.

- Avoid extremes and exaggerations, so as not to arouse mistrust of the opponent and not call into question all your arguments.

Following these rules, you will increase the attention and activity of the interlocutor, minimize the abstractness of your statements, link your arguments much more efficiently and provide maximum understanding of your position.

Communication between two people, when it comes to disputes and discussions, almost always occurs according to the "attacker - defender" scheme. Obviously, you can be in both the first and second positions. Argument constructions are also formed on this principle.

Construction and methods of arguments

There are two main argumentation constructs in total:

- Evidence-based argumentation (used when you need to substantiate or prove something).

- Counterargument (used when it is necessary to refute someone's statements and theses).

To use both designs, it is customary to operate with the same techniques.

Techniques of argument

Whatever your persuasive influence, you should be guided by ten tricks, the use of which optimizes your argument and makes it more effective:

1. **Competence.** Make arguments more objective, reliable and deep.
2. **Visibility.** Make the most of the familiar associations and avoid abstract language.
3. **Clarity.** Link facts and evidence and beware of understatement, confusion, and ambiguity.
4. **The rhythm.** Make your speech more intense as you approach the finale, but do not lose sight of key questions.
5. **The focus.** When discussing something, adhere to a specific course, solve clear problems and strive for clear goals, introducing your opponent in general terms in advance.
6. **The suddenness**. Learn to link facts and details in an unusual and unexpected way and practice using this technique.

7. **Repetition.** Focus the interlocutor on the main ideas and positions, so that the opponent better perceives the information.
8. **Borders.** Define the boundaries of reasoning in advance and do not reveal all the cards in order to maintain a lively conversation and activity of the interlocutor's attention.
9. **Saturation.** When setting out your position, make emotional accents that force your opponent to be as attentive as possible. Do not forget to lower the emotionality as well in order to consolidate the opponent's thoughts and give him and himself a little respite.
10. **Humor and irony.** Be witty and use jokes, but don't be zealous. It is best to act when you need to parry the interlocutor's attacks or express unpleasant arguments for him.

Using these techniques, your argumentative arsenal will be replenished with serious weapons. But, in addition to the methodological aspects, which for the most part relate to the argumentation technique, the art of critical thinking and consistent reasoning is excellently developed by the tactics of argumentation.

Argumentation tactics

Mastering the tactics of argumentation is not as difficult as it might seem. To do this, you just need to learn its basic provisions.

Using arguments

Arguments must begin with confidence. There should be no hesitation. The main arguments are presented at any suitable time, but it is better to do this constantly in a new place.

The choice of technique

The technique should be chosen taking into account the psychological characteristics of the opponent and your own.

Avoiding confrontation

In order for the argumentation phase to proceed normally, one should strive to avoid conflicts and exacerbations, since different positions and forced atmosphere, like a flame, can spread to other areas of communication. And here I have to point out a few nuances:

• Critical issues are considered either at the very beginning or at the very end of the argumentation stage.

- Delicate issues are discussed in private with the interlocutor even before the start of the conversation or discussion, as face-to-face much greater results are achieved than with witnesses.

- When the situation is difficult, there is always a pause, and only after everyone has "let off steam" does communication continue.

Maintaining interest

It is most effective to offer the interlocutor options and information to advance interest in the topic. This means that the current state of affairs is initially described with emphasis on probable negative consequences, and then possible solutions are indicated and their advantages are described in detail.

Two-way argument

With it, you can affect a person whose position does not coincide with yours. You need to point out the pros and cons of your proposal. The effectiveness of this method is affected by the intellectual abilities of the opponent. But, regardless of this, it is necessary to present all the shortcomings that could become known to him from other people and from other sources of information. As for unilateral argumentation, it is applied when the interlocutor has formed his opinion and when he has no objections to your point of view.

The sequence of pros and cons

Based on the conclusions of social psychology, the main formative influence on the opponent's position is provided by such a flow of information, which first lists the positive aspects, and then the negative ones.

Personified argumentation

It is known that the convincingness of facts depends on the perception of people (people, as a rule, are not critical of themselves). Therefore, first of all, you need to try to determine the point of view of the interlocutor, and then insert it into your argument structure. In any case, you should try to avoid contradictory arguments of the opponent and your own argumentation. The easiest way to achieve this is to directly contact your counterpart, for example:

- What do you think about this?
- You're right.
- How do you think this issue can be resolved?

When you admit that your opponent is right and pay attention to him, you will encourage him, which means that he will be more susceptible to your argument.

Drawing conclusions

It happens that the argument is excellent, but the desired goal is not achieved. The reason for this is the inability to generalize information and facts. Based on this, for greater persuasiveness, it is imperative to independently draw conclusions and offer them to the interlocutor. Remember that the facts are not always obvious.

Counterargument

If suddenly you are given arguments that seem to you impeccable, no need to panic. On the contrary, you should remain calm and apply critical thinking:

• Are the facts suggested correct?

• Is it possible to refute this information?

• Is it possible to identify contradictions and inconsistencies in the facts?

• Are the proposed conclusions wrong (at least in part)?

The tactics presented can be the final element of your entire argumentation strategy. And by and large, the information that you met is quite enough to learn how to professionally argue your point of view, position and arguments. But still, this lesson will not be complete unless I give a few more recommendations about convincing arguments - another important element of influencing the opinion of a person and a group of people.

Convincing arguments

What is persuasion? If you do not understand the mass of all kinds of formulations and interpretations, conviction can be called the use of words that will persuade the communication partner to accept your point of view, believe your words or do as you say. And how to achieve this?

The famous American radical organizer and public figure Saul Alinsky created a completely simple theory of persuasion. It says that a person perceives information from the perspective of personal experience. If you try to convey your position to another, not taking into account what he wants to tell you, you may not even count on success. Simply put, if you want to convince someone, you need to give him arguments appropriate to his beliefs, expectations and emotions.

Referring to this, there are four main options for action when arguing:

• Factual data. Despite the fact that sometimes statistics can be wrong, almost always the facts are undeniable. Empirical evidence is considered one of the most convincing tools for compiling the basis of argumentation.

- Emotional impact. As one of the best American psychologists Abraham Maslow said, people respond best when we turn to their emotions, i.e. affect such things as family, love, patriotism, peace, etc. If you want to sound more convincing, you have to express yourself in such a way as to touch your opponent emotions (naturally, within the framework of the rational and preferably in a positive way).

- Personal experience. Stories from one's own life and information verified by personal experience are wonderful tools for influencing the listener. Actually, you yourself can see this for yourself: listen to the person who tells you something "according to the textbook", and then listen to the person who himself experienced or did what he says. Who do you believe more?

- Direct appeal. Of all the existing words, you can choose the one that people never tire of listening to - this is the word "You." Everyone asks himself the question: "What is the use of it for me?" Hence another secret of persuasion: trying to convince someone of something, always put yourself in his place, and when you understand his way of thinking, refer to him using "You" and explain what you need in "his" language.

Surprisingly, these four simplest techniques are not used in life and in work by a huge number of people, in particular those who for some reason belittle the dignity of personalization, appeal to emotions and direct communication with people. But this is a gross mistake, and if you want to become convincing in your words, you should by no means allow it. Combine everything presented in this lesson into a single whole - and you will be amazed at how easily and quickly you can learn to be convincing in any life situation.

The development of critical thinking and argumentation skills will provide you with a huge number of advantages in family, in everyday and professional life. But then again: there are things that can become obstacles in your path. Be aware of the obstacles.

Chapter 13
Analytical Thinking Exercises to Boost Critical Thinking Skills

Exercise 1: Brain Games

Brain games are a fantastic way for you to boost your analytical thinking abilities without having to bore yourself while doing so. There are several games out there that will boost your analytical skills and improve your ability to think critically. These games, from Sudoku to other sorts of word puzzles in which you must unscramble words, can help you figure out how best to think analytically about a situation around you, and you do not even need to go out of your way to find them, either.

If you are reading this, you probably have access to the internet on some sort of device. The internet holds a plethora of information just waiting for you to take advantage of it, and this includes several apps that are designed to help you develop your ability to think analytically. You can download several apps that can help you with this analytical thinking and spend just 10 minutes a day exercising your brain. As you do so, your capacity for analytical thinking will increase. Remember, your brain needs to be exercised just as much as your body, and this is a great way to do so. If you prefer numbers over word games, you could play a game such as Sudoku. If you prefer a word or story game, you could focus on games that are designed around you, solving a mystery.

Exercise 2: Escape Rooms

Yet another way to make this process fun, escape rooms can be a great exercise in ensuring that you strengthen your analytical skills. If you do not know what an escape room is, they are rooms or buildings designed to be like a game—you are locked in for a specific amount of time with no escape, and you have a determined amount of time to solve the puzzle to escape. Along the way, you and a group of people will find all sorts of clues that point you one direction or another, and it will be on you to figure out how best to get through.

These rooms are not particularly easy, though they are fun for those who like games and challenges. You will have to figure out the clues, decipher them, and follow their lead while under the pressure of the clock. However, they are quite enjoyable despite the intense pressure, and if this is your idea of a good time, you can gather up a group of friends and go have fun regularly. Of course, these rooms are not always available, depending on your location. Keep in mind that you may need to travel or may not be able to find one. If you can, however, this is a great and fun way to build up those analytical skills, while possibly having a date night at the same time!

Exercise 3: 10 Minute Learning Period

Every day, challenge yourself to learn something new. Whatever you choose, make sure you spend 10 minutes learning as much as possible about it in order to really help your mind absorb information. Part of being able to analyze comes in the form of being able to also rationalize information quickly and effectively, and sometimes, the best way to do so is through choosing a topic at random and learning as much as you can about it.

Think about it this way—if you have ten minutes to learn everything you need to know about aquariums and how to keep them, what are you going to look at? You need to be able to analyze the information that you know about aquariums already to figure out where your energy is best served. If you do not know the difference between tropical, cold water, and saltwater fish, you are probably not going to spend the entire ten minutes reading about the benefits to the different shapes of tanks and whether you want acrylic, glass, or something else—you would probably look for a beginners guide that would tell you all of the relevant information and start broadly. In starting as broadly as possible, you are able to get the general idea down before you start specializing. After all, knowing the difference between acrylic and a glass tank is not going to help you keep a fish alive.

Exercise 4: Try a New Project

Every now and then, when you have the time to properly invest, try something new. It is good for you to try new things once and a while to break up the monotony of day to day life, but you can also find serious benefits in teaching yourself a new skill suddenly. For example, if you know that you need to be able to multitask, but you have always struggled with it, try learning how to cook a meal that requires plenty of multitasking. You can start with something a bit easier that requires you to cook and prepare two different foods at once, for example, and slowly work your way up.

In choosing a new skill that is something you have little or no experience in, you are forcing your mind to accommodate. You have no choice but to learn the information as quickly as possible, which will force your mind into analysis mode. You will be able to make sure that your mind is focusing on how to get through the skill you have picked up, learning the important information first, which encourages the analysis of information.

Conclusion

Critical thinking helps us to be a better problem solver, we become more aware of what is going on in our surroundings and with this we can protect ourselves from making the wrong decisions based on preconceptions and social standards. With critical thinking, we can get closer to the real solution to problem solving. Critical thinking is really beneficial when we're exposed with too much political propaganda provided by the media today.

Critical thinking is more than just a normal survival thinking of a person. Unfortunately, not everyone is capable to think critically. Some people are not as open minded as the others, however, it can be learned. Anyone can practice critical thinking as long as they are interested to so do.

The "thinking" in critical thinking can have some instinctive activity, as well, but it significantly consist of the mental or intellectual aptitudes at absorbing and processing knowledge, details, and circumstances of any kind. One is considered successful at this once he can essentially express the different components of the problem there is, including the acknowledgment of the problem, the different applicable details, a solution, and explanation for everything. It's very difficult always put feelings into words, but you can put critical thoughts into words easily.

Therefore, critical thinking is thought-provoking job and this really requires unpretentious skill, although for some people, it seems very effortless. Inborn skills are useful, but skills that can be learned are important, too.

In order to recognize in effective means, to make intelligent and innate connections, to process data, to question the different aspects of a problem, to see different sides of reality and of what it may be, to progress reasonably among abundant thoughts, to articulate an insight or resolution, and to answer the question "why?" something has happened. Critical thinking is suitably involved in almost every sensible endeavor of life.

Being creative means surrounding yourself with ideas. Those ideas come from all different sources. The artist may be inspired by his surroundings. The grandmother may be inspired by tradition and ideas from her past. Find out what inspires you and surround yourself with it, whether in scrapbook format or in a specially created craft room.

Everyone finds creativity when they take the time to look at an object and see the seed for a creative idea. That seed is wasted if no one sees the potential, though by opening up your mind to this potential, your imagination will help you to be creative. This, in turn, will give you the feeling of achievement that creative people feel. Try it. It really will boost your self-assurance and your feeling at one with life.

Eventually, people have to realize and understand that creativity is not something that they can simply hope for. Creativity is a life's worth of hard work and perseverance. You have to find within yourself what it is you really want to create. You have to constantly be aware that creativity is something you should develop.

It's a given from birth, yes, but without proper honing, creativity is a gift that dies out. And when it dies, it's a big shame. There are millions of things creativity can offer people. All we have to do for it in return is to keep nurturing it via endlessly looking for ideas that will excite the world and that will keep the passion within you burning and your creativity flowing.

So, why critical thinking should be part of everyone's life? It is for the reason that with this, we can engage all the aspects of life efficiently; you have to be somewhat capable and competent. Life always comes complicated, but the good thing is that it's not impossible to manage it in order. And it has to be betrothed. Avoiding the disorderliness of life instead of resolving it is a sign of personal problem. But, to deal with life completely, to accept reality in an intelligent and healthy way, and to fight with it–that is how everyone should deal with life! Critical thinking pursues wisdom, and wisdom and healthy life always set off.

The path to creativity was never an easy one but with passion, a focused mind, and a brave heart, anyone can transform a clever idea into a brilliant outcome.

www.ingramcontent.com/pod-product-compliance
Lightning Source LLC
Chambersburg PA
CBHW070635220526
45466CB00001B/177